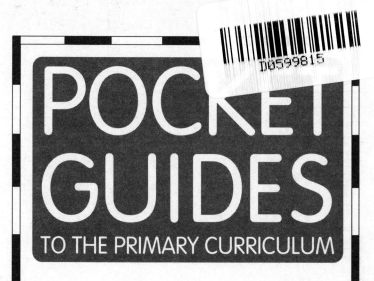

POCKET GUIDES

TO THE PRIMARY CURRICULUM

History

Paul Noble

Provides the knowledge you need
to teach the primary curriculum

Author
Paul Noble

Editor
Jean Coppendale

Assistant Editor
David Sandford

Cover design
Joy Monkhouse
Rachel Warner

Designers
Mickey Pledge
Lynda Murray
Sarah Rock

Illustrations
Garry Davies
Neil Gower

Cover photograph
Calvin Hewitt

Published by Scholastic Ltd,
Villiers House,
Clarendon Avenue,
Leamington Spa,
Warwickshire CV32 5PR

Text © 2001 Paul Noble
© 2001 Scholastic Ltd

1 2 3 4 5 6 7 8 9 0   1 2 3 4 5 6 7 8 9 0

British Library Cataloguing-in-
Publication Data
A catalogue record for this book is
available from the British Library.

ISBN 0-439-01746-7

CONTENTS

History

Introduction

Scholastic *Pocket Guides* aim to give you a user-friendly summary of the basic information that will help you to teach the National Curriculum. This volume covers primary history – that is, history at both Key Stage 1 and Key Stage 2 – and it contains enough information to support your teaching of history right through primary school. It may, in fact, include more than you actually need, because the curriculum allows you some choices.

The revised National Curriculum implemented in September 2000 follows the pattern of previous versions of the Programme of Study for History. For example, at Key Stage 2 children have to study one world history topic from a list of seven. From those on the list, Ancient Egypt and the Aztecs have proved to be the most popular with teachers since the National Curriculum started and so both topics are included here.

Similarly for Key Stage 1, examples of some possible infant study topics are suggested here, together with the sorts of questions that might be asked in order to bring a proper historical focus to a topic that will almost certainly have a strong cross-curricular feel to it. We have chosen to look at the possibilities presented by studying 'homes' and another popular topic, 'holidays'.

For older infants the choice widens even further as the curriculum takes on a more discrete historical feel. Famous individuals in history can be studied; in this guide you will be directed to particular people within our chosen event (the Great Fire of London), but you may find it helpful to examine the links to other Key Stage 2 topics when you are seeking suitable subjects to study, for example Florence Nightingale and Victorian Britain (see page 161) or Alfred the Great and Anglo-Saxon Britain (see page 93). The choice of individuals might also be driven by the local history focus at Key Stage 2. This will, of course, depend on what is available in your area.

In this book, all the compulsory topics at Key Stage 2 are covered, as well as the most popular options. Where an overview of several topics is specifically required, as with Romans, Anglo-Saxons and Vikings, for example, this is given at the start of the first chapter. Whichever group of invaders you choose to study, they must be set within the context of the whole series of invasions that took place in Britain during the first millennium.

The Programme of Study for Primary History comprises two main elements. First there is a requirement for knowledge, skills and understanding, and secondly for breadth of study, which provides the experiences and contexts in which the former are to be taught – that is, the historical content. The requirements are summarized below, but for the full details you should refer to your copy of the History Curriculum published by the QCA.

Knowledge, skills and understanding
● Chronological understanding (time, dates and the language of time).
● Knowledge and understanding of events, people and changes in the past (includes causes, outcomes, differences and similarities).
● Historical interpretation (includes reasons for different representations of the past at Key Stage 2).
● Historical enquiry (evidence, how to use and select it).
● Organization and communication (the recall and communication of history).

Breadth of Study (Key Stage 1)

● Changes in their own lives and the way of life of their family or others around them.

● The way of life of people in the more distant past who lived in the local area or elsewhere in Britain.

● The lives of significant men, women and children drawn from the history of Britain and the wider world.

● Past events from the history of Britain and the wider world.

Breadth of Study (Key Stage 2)

Three British studies

● An overview of Roman, Anglo-Saxon and Viking invasion and settlement.

A study of one of these three topics in depth:

● Britain and the wider world in Tudor times

● Victorian Britain

● Britain since 1930.

A European history study

● Ancient Greece.

A world history study (one of the following)

● Ancient Egypt*

● Ancient Sumer

● The Assyrian Empire

● The Indus Valley

● The Maya

● Benin

● The Aztecs*.

*These topics are covered in this book.

The study of history is fascinating mainly because it is about people, and nothing interests us more than ourselves. However, history is not about learning everything about the past, for the past is huge and ultimately unknowable and we can only create our own partial view of it based upon evidence. So do not expect to be able to teach your children everything about the Romans or the Victorians – this cannot be done. Similarly, this book cannot include all the information that is known about these topics – we have made a careful selection of what to cover, just as you must do. Remember, focus on people and tell stories that will grip the children's imaginations, because ultimately it is with our imaginations that we really comprehend truth.

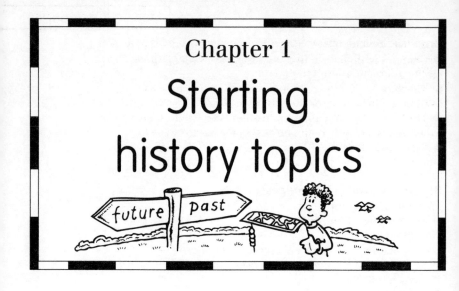

Chapter 1
Starting history topics

Unlike most of the other chapters in this book, this chapter does not contain a solid body of knowledge to be covered. There are no lists of facts to be learned nor dates to be remembered.

Children of infant school age are at a very early stage on the path to historical understanding. Facts, dates and judgements – the very stuff of academic history – are comparatively unimportant, as well as nigh on incomprehensible, to very young children. These children are getting ready to explore the past and you must chiefly be concerned with preparing the way for that future learning and understanding.

Before they can do anything else, young children need to understand that the past exists, that it is big, and that it is separate from the present. In Reception and Year 1, teachers must lead children to this understanding and start to provide them with the language and vocabulary to enable them to talk about the past and begin a tentative exploration of it. As a result, the approach in this chapter must be different from that used in others.

What areas of study?

Children need to acquire the knowledge, skills and understanding specified in the National Curriculum, and to do this we need to focus on particular areas of study. At the beginning of Key Stage 1, children are expected to study

personally related history ('changes in their own lives and
the way of life of their family or others around them') and
for this there are many suitable topics.

In this chapter 'holidays' and 'homes' are used to provide
examples of such topics. However, it must be stressed that
there are many other equally convenient topic 'bags' into
which National Curriculum requirements will readily fit.
For example:

Toys
Shops and shopping
School
Growing up in the past
When teacher (or other suitable adult) was young
*People who help us – using a 'then and now' theme, such
as firemen, policemen, doctors, nurses, postmen, milkmen*
Life on a farm
Great grandad (or grandma)
Children's games.

You might also choose to study a famous person, although
many schools elect to do this in Year 2 and link it with the
study of a particular historical event. The more general
topics listed above are well suited to Reception and Year 1,
although the names of famous people can arise naturally
during other work, as well as during national
commemorations or anniversaries.

People who might make a suitable subject for study are:

Amy Johnson
Sir Robert Baden-Powell
Queen Elizabeth the Queen Mother
The Venerable Bede
Captain Scott of the Antarctic
George Frideric Handel
Vincent Van Gogh

The list is almost endless. Look for local connections and
check the local paper and your diary. Other excellent
sources are the historical topics chosen for the end of Key
Stage 1. For example, from the period of the Great Fire of
London you could study Samuel Pepys, Sir Christopher
Wren or Charles II. If you are still searching for suitable
people, look at the topics for Key Stage 2: each one has key
figures worthy of study, although, bearing in mind the age
of the children, look for strong storylines that will appeal to
the children. For example, you might consider Florence

Nightingale, David Livingstone, Hereward the Wake, Queen Boudica or Queen Elizabeth I.

Approaching the subject facts

How you bring the subject facts to the children's attention is more important than the facts themselves. Select a simple question and then set out to answer it. (This approach should be continued for any historical study – at Key Stage 2 the children can come up with their own questions to which they wish to find answers.)

The broader the question, the more complex the answer: compare 'What were holidays like in the past?' with 'What was it like to go on holiday when grandma was a child?' The latter is a better question for young children to tackle: it is more precise, more manageable and more understandable to the child.

Holidays

Subject facts

A sensible starting point for this topic is the child's own experience of a holiday, so it is a good topic with which to start the new school year. You will need to build up strong images of the children's holidays and a bank of pictures, objects and stories to use for comparative work.

Choose also a period in the past that is within the living memory of adults for comparison. Children do not have a precise vocabulary for measuring time so there is no need to be pedantic about this. You may opt to use holiday experiences from a number of different decades – within living memory is best, although given sufficient resources, you could focus on the Edwardian or late Victorian period.

Keep the project focus simple, using the 'question' approach mentioned above. For example:

> *What was it like to go on holiday in those days?*
> *How did people (for example, grandma) travel?*
> *How did they enjoy themselves?*
> *Where did they go?*
> *What is the same/different about then and now?*

If you were to choose, for example, the 1950s as the period of comparison, you would need to establish in your own mind the historical context and learn a few relevant facts (unless you are of a certain age).

The seaside in the 1950s

Children in the 1950s were mostly experiencing the seaside and holidays for the first time. As with bananas and white bread, they had been denied these pleasures during wartime. The war was still very close in people's memories.

Meteor jet fighters of the RAF routinely 'buzzed' the holiday beaches as a way of showing the flag and boosting civilian morale, which in spite of the end of the war was still quite low. Some wartime restrictions, such as rationing, lingered on. However, the 1950s were a period of high employment and growing affluence; Harold Macmillan's famous 'You've never had it so good' speech was made in 1959. Between 1951 and 1955 wages rose by 20 per cent in real terms and one of the first priorities for people spending this money was holidays.

Bank holidays marked an even bigger exodus from the cities than today. Massive traffic jams occurred on the Exeter bypass and on the way to the Lake District. Coach and rail excursions were provided especially to cater for the trip to the seaside.

On arriving at the seaside, holiday-makers often found neglected promenades and piers – little had changed since the Edwardian era. The detritus of war was still visible in the early 1950s, especially along the eastern and southern coasts, and children would often clamber over abandoned gun emplacements without any real knowledge of what they were. Fairgrounds contained rifle ranges, coconut shies and 'What the butler saw' peep-shows, mostly of pre-war origin. (The ladies undressing in the latter were usually Edwardian – I know, I saw what the Butler saw!) Fish and chip lunches, whelks and cockles, end of pier concerts, a look through a penny telescope, ice creams and sticks of rock, candyfloss and Punch and Judy shows were the main attractions. Walking along the promenade was popular with the older generation, perhaps visiting the town gardens, a waxwork display or listening to a band concert. The package holiday industry had not developed and many people stayed in cheap lodgings, caravans or chalets, or camped.

Why you need to know these facts

Young children need to learn that the past is different from the present, and should have opportunities to ask questions about the information given to them about the past.

Amazing facts

● The average weekly wage was £11 7s 10d in 1955 yet people still found money for a holiday – but rarely was that holiday taken abroad.

Teaching ideas

● Tell the Punch and Judy story. Make or play with puppets (or both).

● Make a list of all the games that you might play on the beach today. Compare them with the chosen period. What did people do in past times?

● Collect pictures of all the ways in which people may travel to their holiday destination. Use 'then and now' comparisons.

● Invite an elderly person to come in and describe a journey to the seaside when he or she was little.

● Make a list of all the things sold on a beach. Use 'then and now' comparisons.

● Dress children up in holiday clothes. (You could do this on a dummy or mock-up picture on the wall.) How do the children's clothes compare with, for example, 1950s Fair Isle pullovers, scarves, snake buckle belts, National Health spectacles or woollen swimsuits (no bikinis)?

● Make a bar chart showing the different ways in which the class travelled to their holiday destinations. Compare this with great-grandad's time.

● Use pictures or words to sequence the main events in a journey to a holiday destination then and now. Ask the children to order and re-order the words or pictures.

● Collect and display holiday memorabilia. Discuss or show 'then and now' differences.

● Make a 'holidays in the past' display. You could start with photographs of adults and then put information about their holiday experiences as a child underneath the picture.

● There are many possible links with other subjects and topics. You might consider looking at sand and its uses, the qualities of wet and dry sand, the biblical story of the man who built his house upon sand, floating and sinking, pebbles, stones and shells, seashore animals, travel, places on a map and so on.

Homes

Subject facts

This topic is about homes, not houses, so remember to link the work you do to the lives of the people who live or have lived in the buildings you study. This should be a cross-curricular project well-suited to the very youngest children.

Begin by looking at how houses are built – building sites fascinate most children. Try to arrange a visit to one (there should be an opportunity for health and safety work here). Most of the project should be a 'then and now' comparison. It will be more interesting if you choose a particular person or home to study. (Sensitivity will be needed in approaching this topic; think before you enquire too deeply.)

Use the question approach as before, for example:

What was it like to live in (your grandparents') home?
What did the furniture look like?
What equipment did they use in the kitchen?
How did they amuse themselves at home in the evenings?
Did their house have double glazing, central heating, television and so on?

Why you need to know these facts

At Key Stage 1, the historical focus should be on people's lives and lifestyles. A study of homes will provide invaluable clues to life in the recent past and give lots of opportunities to compare 'now' and 'then'.

Amazing facts

● 100 000 London homes were destroyed by bombs in the Second World War.
● Bricks used to be all sorts of sizes until standard dimensions were established about 100 years ago.
● People have lived in houses for about 10 000 years. Buildings made of mud bricks dating from around 8000 years ago have been discovered in Catal in Turkey.

● Talk about the difference between a house and a home.
● Make a chart of words that describe the homes of different people (you might like to include animals as well).
● Make a bar chart showing the types of homes lived in by children in the class. You could make a comparative chart showing the types of homes lived in by their grandparents. Compare the charts and discuss.
● Look at how a house is made. Invite someone in to talk to the class about building a house.
● Collect poems and stories about houses and homes ('The House that Jack Built', 'The Three Little Pigs').
● Make a photographic display of the homes that the children live in. (Be sensitive; it might be best to stick to the exterior of houses for this exercise.)
● Make a plan (or model) on which the children can place a representation of their own home. In a village this might take the form of a village map.
● Construct a timeline on which you put a named house picture (for each child) roughly in order of the date that they were constructed. The children will have to do some detective work at home. (Don't become obsessed with dates, it is sequence that is needed. For example, Mary's house is older than Jo's. Nathaniel's house is the oldest. Imran lives in a brand new house.)
● Make a display or class book of time-related words (old, older, before, after and so on). This might be illustrated in some way to indicate meaning.
● Collect words that describe the buildings that people live in: words such as house, cottage, bungalow, flat, penthouse, semi-detached, detached, terraced, hut, mansion, chalet and so on.
● Make an illustrated dictionary of words that describe the different parts of a house (for example gutter, rendering, porch, lintel, loft and so on).
● Focus on one house (say from the 1950s) and try to imagine who lived there in the past. If you have grandparents who used to live there it will help. How did they live? What did their furniture look like? You could do a large wall display of the work.
● Have a 1950s evening. Listen to the wireless, read books, eat snacks or sweets available then and so on. Dress up in appropriate clothes if possible. You could do similar exercises for an Edwardian home – sing round the piano, sew, knit, read and so on.
● Use a doll's house as the central feature of a study of homes. Name the parts of the house, look at each room in

turn, furnish and decorate it. You could start from scratch with a doll's house constructed from boxes and build it up as the project progresses.

Resources

The secret of success when sourcing history projects for very young children is knowing when to stop. If you are not careful you will overwhelm your class with material, and the children will not focus on anything sufficiently to make sense of it. So, although there is a list of resources here, be confident that you can select and use a few items to their best advantage.

First there are the objects that the children can bring to the project. For **Holidays** you should display and use a selection of holiday photographs from family albums – my holiday, mum's holiday when she was a girl, great-grandma's trip to the seaside and so on. Catalogues from travel agents provide useful material, and copies of old travel posters are good for comparative work (old steam railway posters provide particularly useful talking points). Holiday souvenirs are also fun to discuss – always remember that you are looking for 'then and now' comparisons. You might be lucky to have some old holiday clothes brought in to school. Great-grandad's knitted swimming trunks, perhaps? (One grandparent arrived with a motorbike and sidecar to show the vehicle his wife and family used in the 1950s to go on holiday.) Whatever you get, use it – it has a real hands-on quality that is worth a thousand words.

For **Homes** the artefacts are likely to be easy to handle. A 'tinkering table' is ideal, but only put objects on the table that are virtually indestructible or you may be in trouble. Choosing 'Great-grandma's time' for comparison will probably yield the best trawl, although you may be surprised at how few ordinary day-to-day objects from that period there are about – people only tend to save the precious. Would you expect to get for comparison a 1950s iron, a television, some ceramic ducks, a roll of wallpaper, a 78rpm record, a wooden tennis racket or an ancient copy of the *Radio Times*? You can only ask and hope. Photographs and pictures are again a vital resource and you should be able to find plenty for the children to examine. (See the book list overleaf.)

As everything needs to be as 'hands-on' as possible, make sure that you use people as much as you can. An elderly cleaner, retired milkman, great grandad, or ex-teacher can be a real boon. Select a good volunteer and make the most of him or her. The chief advantage is that the children can interact with the visitor, ask questions and talk. Give the visitor a precise brief but don't arrange a lecture. Let the children set the pace.

Your young children need to be shown that the past existed, so a visit to the park/school/shop that grandma used, or to the now defunct railway station or track, or a session in a local or other relevant museum is important. Alongside this must go pictures – use photographs, films, slides, posters and videos.

Recommended background reading and books with ideas and teaching strategies:

History 5 to 9 by Joan Blyth (Hodder and Stoughton) – strong on techniques and resources but biased towards the higher age group.
A Teacher's Guide to... series (English Heritage) This ever-expanding series of concise and colourful A4 booklets contains a number of useful titles for Key Stage 1 teachers. Particularly recommended are *Learning from Objects; Using Listed Buildings; Using School Buildings* (the focus may be slightly off our topics, but they contain relevant ideas and wise suggestions) and *Using Portraits*. A full catalogue of English Heritage resources, including videos and posters, can be obtained from English Heritage Education, Freepost 22 (WD214), London (Tel: 020 7973 3442). The website is www.english-heritage.org.uk.

Useful practical ideas can be found in the following publications:

Primary Teacher Yearbooks: Teaching Reception, Teaching Year One, Teaching Year Two (three titles) (Scholastic).
Starting History, Skills Pack (Collins) – includes all the photographs of household objects that you need.
Cross Curricular Big Book (Collins) – teacher's notes and sturdy large pictures with some 'then and now' comparisons.
Houses and Places of Worship Resource Pack (Collins).

Books for children

Story and picture books should be one of your best resources. You will find useful books amongst your reading scheme books as well as on the library shelves. Sift and sort them, then make a display or arrange a special 'topic book corner'. Here are just a few examples:

Beside the Sea Roy and Jean Gerrard (Gollanz) – lovely pictures and a rhyming text.

And Miss Carter Wore Pink Helen Bradley (Jonathan Cape) – wonderful source to be dipped into, it focuses on the Edwardian period but is relevant beyond this.

Annabel's House Norman Messenger (Dorling Kindersley) – although it focuses on the Edwardian period, this could easily be used for a later period without the moveable people – a wonderful picture book.

Wilfrid Gordon McDonald Partridge Mem Fox (Puffin) – a marvellous, touching story about memories – compulsory reading.

Good Girl Granny Pat Thomson and Faith Jaques, (Gollanz) – just what you need as support for either topic, shows how the elderly can distort their memories of the past.

From Me to You Paul Rogers (Orchard) – touching story, links the past to the present.

Grandpa John Burningham (Puffin) – one of many books about grandparents, all useful when trying to link the past to the child's experience of the present.

Collecting

Most infant teachers are hoarders and it is a habit worth cultivating. Look out particularly for picture postcards when you are on holiday or visiting a museum. Build up your own project pack for the history topic you are studying.

Visits

For topics such as these, a journey to a special museum is not really recommended unless it is on your doorstep. *The National Museum of Photography, Film and Television* in Bradford is wonderful for 1950s TV, for example, but for this age group a local museum or a walk down the local high street would be more advisable, unless you live in Bradford. There are also some wonderful transport museums, including *The Crich Tramway Museum*, Derbyshire, where you can ride on a tram, *The Black Country Museum*, Dudley, and *The Beamish Industrial Museum*, County Durham – but distance may rule these out.

Chapter 2
The Great Fire of London

The Great Fire of London in 1666 destroyed a huge part of the largely wooden medieval city of London. In doing so, it helped to remove some of the areas that had been breeding grounds for the Great Plague that had decimated the city the year before. As a result of the fire, the city was rebuilt to new standards, although somewhat below the visionary levels proposed by some architects of the time. However, London emerged with a new cathedral, 52 new churches and some healthier, safer housing.

Introducing the Great Fire

	Event timeline
	Sunday 2nd September 1666
Midnight	*The fire begins in a baker's oven at the end of Pudding Lane, not far from the Tower of London.*
3.00am	*Samuel Pepys is woken by a maid who tells him about the fire.*
Dawn	*The fire has already destroyed over 300 houses and is still burning.*

Sunday 2nd September 1666 (cont.)

Later in the day Pepys reports to King Charles II and the Duke of York and advises that houses in front of the fire should be pulled down to stop it spreading further. Pepys goes to see the Lord Mayor to command him what to do, but finds that the Mayor is exhausted and overwhelmed by the situation. By the afternoon large numbers of people are fleeing by road and river. Attempts to stop the fire are having no effect.

Midday

Pepys' own house is threatened so he removes his belongings and buries some of his valuables in the garden.

Nightfall

Monday 3rd

The Fire is at its peak, fanned by strong winds and helped by the presence of so much combustible material. The Duke of York rides around the city accompanied by his guard to maintain calm. Many country people arrive with carts to help evacuate the population to the surrounding villages. That night St Paul's Cathedral catches fire. Eyewitness accounts report 10 000 houses burning at one time and a smoke cloud an estimated 90km (56 miles) in length.

Tuesday 4th

Molten lead from St Paul's roof is running down the street. The Old Bailey and Newgate Prison burn. Late in the day, the wind begins to abate. Houses are blown up to clear the ground in front of the fire.

4pm

Wednesday 5th

The King orders food supplies to be brought in to feed the homeless. More men are brought in to blow up houses in the path of the fire. The fire begins to come under control. Over 200 000 refugees are camped in the fields of Highgate and Islington.

Thursday 6th

The fire still burns, but less fiercely.

Friday 7th

Samuel Pepys gets up in the morning and finds that the fire is out.

The heat of the ashes can still be felt months later.

Why do we need to know about the Great Fire?

Very young children do not need to know too many details about the event, as this will confuse them. For example, many children will be unable to cope with a four-figure number and for them, the use of numerical dating will not mean very much. The children do need to know:

● the main events of the Fire
● significant figures involved in the event (Samuel Pepys, King Charles II, the Mayor of London)
● why the Fire started, how it spread, how it was put out
● the effects of the fire upon people and property
● that the Fire happened a long time ago (the event could be placed in relation to other events in history, for example after the Romans, before trains were invented)
● that we know about the Fire through eyewitness accounts.

The story of the Fire

This topic is appropriate for Year 2 children who love stories. It is best to tell it rather than read it, but the following outline could be expanded or modified to suit your taste and needs. The facts are all true.

---

*A long time ago, a **very** long time ago. Long before you were born, there was a fire.*

It was no ordinary fire.

This was a giant monster of a fire, one that ate everything in its way – houses, churches, even the tall steeple of a great cathedral reaching up into the sky. This fire devoured them all. Nothing was safe from it.

It began like this.

Thomas Faryner was a hard-working baker. He had been baking bread all day and was feeling very hot. His oven was hot, his bakery was hot, and the streets outside the bakery were also hot. There had been no rain for weeks. The thatched roofs of the wooden houses were crisp and dry, and the narrow streets of London were sun-baked and dusty.

This all made Thomas feel extra weary and he was really looking forward to going to bed. He quickly raked out the fire in the bread oven, and went upstairs.

He did not sleep for long as he was woken by shouting.

'Fire! Fire!' He quickly jumped out of bed but found that choking smoke blocked the stairs. As fast as he could he looked for another way to escape. Together with his wife and a servant, he climbed out through the bedroom window and on to the roof. 'Help!' they shouted, as loudly as they could.

Soon all the neighbours were out in the street and they were able to climb across the rooftops to safety. Sadly, that was the end of the bakery – but it was just the beginning of the Great Fire.

Later in the night someone woke the Mayor of London and told him that a large part of London was on fire. He looked out of his bedroom window. 'Tish! A woman could put it out!' he said, and went back to bed.

At 3 o'clock in the morning a servant woke Samuel Pepys, an important man who worked for the king. He thought that the fire was too far off to worry about, and he too went back to bed.

But the next morning Samuel Pepys decided to walk to the city to have a closer look. He found that the fire had already destroyed hundreds of houses and was burning more fiercely every minute. A wind was blowing strongly, and the flames were roaring, like a dragon's breath, leaping from house to house and devouring everything.

Samuel Pepys immediately went to see the king and told him to pull down the houses in front of the fire so that the dragon would have nothing to feed on and would die. King Charles II commanded this to be done.

Pepys then went to see the mayor to give him the king's orders, but by this time the mayor was a frightened man. He had been trying hard to fight the fire and was exhausted. There were tears in his eyes.

'What can I do? What can I do?' he cried.

The fire burned all day Sunday and Monday and on into Tuesday. Thousands of people fled from their homes,

*trying to carry all their precious possessions with them.
Some escaped down the River Thames in boats and
barges. Furniture and clothes that these people had to
leave behind floated in the river.*

*Pepys again went to report to the king. The rich people
did not want to have their houses pulled down and were
holding up the battle against the monster fire. The poor
would not leave their houses until the flames actually
caught hold. Even the pigeons did not want to leave.
Some birds stayed too long, and as they flew up to escape
the flames, their wings were singed so they could not fly,
and they plummeted to their deaths below.*

*Pepys told the king that more men were needed to pull
the houses down more quickly. So workers were brought
from the dockyards and soldiers came to help fight the
fire with a new weapon – gunpowder. Soon the air was
filled with loud explosions. Boom! Bang! Crash! Some
people panicked. They thought that they could hear
cannons and that London was being attacked. But
houses were being blown up before the fire could eat
them and so, as the wind began to drop, the fight against
the fire began to be won.*

*But it was not quite over. Newgate Prison caught fire. So
did the law courts and, worst of all, so did the great
cathedral of St Paul's. The metal on its roof melted with
the heat and the hot metal ran down the streets like
water. The ground near the fire was too hot to walk on
and smoke covered the sun.*

*By Friday it was clear that the Great Fire of London was
out, although firefighters went round with buckets of
water putting out the burning embers for days
afterwards. And for a long time there was a strange glow
in the sky as the ash cloud was blown high over London.*

*The fire taught a number of lessons. People learned to
build houses that were made of brick and that would not
burn easily. And Thomas Faryner learned that when you
put out a fire, no matter how tired you are, you must
make sure that you put it out properly. Otherwise...*

How do we know about the Great Fire?

Most of the evidence is documentary. There are many letters, maps, diaries and plans relating to the fire and to the rebuilding of London. Samuel Pepys and John Evelyn kept diaries, but many other people wrote about the event including William Burnett (later Bishop of Salisbury), the Earl of Clarendon, William Denton (one of the king's doctors) and William Taswell (a schoolboy at the time). The *London Gazette* gave the official account and there are some splendidly detailed maps from the period which show the extent of the fire. Documents and accounts of the planning and building works after the fire that can also be consulted. In the Museum of London, the hoses, helmets and buckets used by the firefighters can be seen. St Paul's Cathedral is also, in a way, evidence of the fire. Designed by Sir Christopher Wren, it was built to replace the medieval cathedral, which was destroyed in the conflagration. He also designed 51 new churches for the burned-out city.

What happened after the fire?

The cost to property was enormous. Out of London's 109 churches, 87 were destroyed. It consumed 151 hectares (373 acres) within the walls of the City of London, and some 13 200 houses. The total cost was estimated at £10 million (London's annual income was £12 000 at the time). One huge loss was in books and paper as all the warehouses and booksellers were destroyed near St Paul's, as were the many books that had been stored in the cathedral for safety. These were all destroyed at an estimated value of £2 million.

Thomas Faryner, the baker in Pudding Lane where the fire started, claimed that he had raked out his oven fires and that the fire had definitely been started on purpose. Although during the fire it was believed that it was started deliberately (by the Dutch or the French), an inquiry afterwards found that the cause was accidental.

Many plans were put forward for the rebuilding of the City of London but none was adopted. The Rebuilding Act of 1667 decreed that the City should be rebuilt upon the old street plan. However, great care was taken to use less-combustible materials such as brick and stone, and the new buildings made London a safer and healthier place. The Act also laid down strict rules about how buildings should be constructed.

A monument (designed by Sir Christopher Wren) was erected close to the site of the start of the fire.

Why you need to know these facts

At Key Stage 1, children have to study a past event. Our choice is the Great Fire of London because it was an important event, and was commemorated by a famous memorial (the monument designed by Sir Christopher Wren, and completed in 1677). The Fire is an exciting story that can be understood at a simple level and will appeal to young children. It provides ample opportunity for developing the kind of knowledge, skills and understanding defined in the Key Stage 1 Programme of Study for History.

Amazing facts

● Only one person is known with certainty to have been killed by the Fire.

Common misconceptions

The newly invented fire engines were crucial in putting out the fire.
Of course, every little helped, but the much-vaunted arrival of fire engines, quite unlike those we know today, were helpless in the face of such a fierce conflagration. The fire was defeated by a combination of dramatic measures (blowing up houses in the path of the fire and using additional troops) and luck, as the wind that fanned the flames died down.

● Write out some sentences outlining the main events of the fire and cut them out. The children could work in groups to sequence the sentences correctly. This could be made less difficult by using illustrations instead of, or to complement, the text.

● The children could work in groups and construct a class frieze of the Great Fire, based on contemporary engravings (widely reprinted in books on the period). This could be done effectively using silhouettes of buildings, red paper and cotton wool for flames and smoke.

● Design a newspaper front page about the fire.

● Invite representatives from your local fire station to pay the school a visit and talk about their job.

● Work as a class to make a list of fire safety rules that would have helped to prevent the Great Fire of London. Tour the school examining your own fire precautions.

● Build models of the kind of wood framed houses that were burned in the fire.

Samuel Pepys

Subject facts

Samuel Pepys only kept his famous diary for nine years, from 1660 to 1669. He stopped writing when his wife died and his eyesight began to fail.

The diary gives a vivid account of court intrigues and the problems Pepys experienced in naval administration – matters that he was deeply concerned about. It also gives an insight into the attitudes and culture of the time and, of course, a wonderful eyewitness account of the events of the Great Fire of London. The diary was written in a sort of mixture of code and shorthand to protect it from prying eyes. In it, Pepys was frank about his personal liaisons and feelings.

Pepys was an intelligent, educated man with considerable ability as an administrator and musician. His father was a London tailor but his father's cousin was the Earl of Sandwich, and it was with his help that Pepys got a job as a secretary to the Admiralty. His ability secured him promotion, although his supposed involvement in treasonable plots and corruption twice lost him his job. But Pepys was a survivor, and he rose to an important position in the Admiralty where he was hard-working and efficient. He was made President of the Royal Society in 1684.

In their own words

> *But Lord! What a sad sight it was by moonlight to see the whole City almost on fire – that you might see it plain at Woolwich as if you were by it.*
> Samuel Pepys' Diary

Why you need to know these facts

Samuel Pepys is a 'significant' person from the past. His story is one that the children can readily respond to. They can also understand and ask questions about the main sources of our knowledge of his life.

Teaching ideas

● Imitate Samuel Pepys. Write a diary of the events of the fire, pretending that you are a character living in London at the time – a maid, a firefighter, the Lord Mayor or a country visitor.
● The children could act out some of the events of the fire. Each group could be given the task of making a play of an aspect of the fire – the beginning, firefighters, refugees, Samuel Pepys and the Mayor, and the end. These could be performed as a class assembly.
● Samuel Pepys dug a deep hole to bury some of his valued possessions, including wine and Parmesan cheese. Ask the children to write about the precious things that they would hide if disaster threatened and also to explain their choices.

Resources

There is a lot of reference material about the fire available, but you do need to look beyond history books alone.

You can glean ideas from an English Heritage video made for INSET *The Key Stage 1 Curriculum* (ref: XT11513), which follows a project that includes a visit to a 17th century house. Also from English Heritage, *Using the Evidence of the Historic Environment* (ref: XP 14001) is a book containing ideas for Key Stage 1.

Books
For this project, books about London can provide useful contextual information, for example *Kid's London* (Dorling

Kindersley Travel Guides). You could put up a display of maps – one to show where London is, and another to show where the fire started and the extent of the damage. (Bear in mind that a child's understanding of maps is very limited at this age.)

Books about firemen abound for infants, and some contain information about fighting fires in the past. If you want to broaden the scope of the topic, or give it a more cross-curricular feel, then these books will be invaluable.

As for the event itself, the majority of information books are aimed at Key Stage 2, but children of this age need a lot of visual material, so do not dismiss books just because the text is too advanced. You will need lots of pictures of London, of wood-framed houses and of 17th century streets and people.

The Stuart period was removed from Key Stage 2 history a few years ago, so much excellent material has gone out of print. But if you can find some of the Key Stage 2 textbooks produced at the time, they contain a lot of useable material on the Great Fire. The BBC has made some excellent dramatized programmes on the Plague and the Great Fire (*Landmarks* series). All these may be available via your local library or museum resource service.

If you want more background information yourself, or eyewitness accounts to quote to children, then the following are excellent – they also contain many contemporary and other pictures:

The Great Fire of London Gustav Milne (Historical Publications Ltd) – a very comprehensive account

Plague and Fire Leonard Cowie (Wayland) – more accessible than the above, a blow-by-blow account

The Illustrated Pepys Robert Latham (Bell & Hyman) – selections from Pepys' *Diary*; the famous descriptions with pictures.

Visits

If your school is within the London area, then a visit to the Museum of London (tel: 020 7600 3699), or a trip up the Fire Monument is worth considering (but remember it has 311 steps!). If you are inexperienced at planning historical trips with young children, then do take advice. In general, the further the trip, the less advised it is to make it.

Chapter 3

Ancient Egypt

The key to understanding Egypt is the River Nile. Its fertile flood plain has supported the lives of settlers for over 5000 years of recorded history. The Nile delta (Lower Egypt) in the north is where the early Egyptian civilization advanced most rapidly. The narrower Nile valley that stretched southwards was called Upper Egypt.

The world's longest river, the Nile runs for 6738km (4187 miles). It gave birth to the civilization of Ancient Egypt, a civilization that lasted to the time of Roman rule in 30BC, a period of some 3000 years.

Introducing Ancient Egypt

Subject facts

Who were the Ancient Egyptians?

The people whom we usually refer to as Ancient Egyptians date from the time when the Lower and Upper parts of Egypt were united by Menes, the king of Upper Egypt, in around 3100BC. At the junction of the two united lands Menes established his capital city, later called Memphis.

The first settlements around the River Nile, about a quarter of a million years ago, were probably just small hunting camps. But by 3500bc, the people of Lower and Upper Egypt were developing separately, and it seems that in Lower Egypt the people had discovered how to build structures that we would recognize as houses.

Timeline	
Lower and Upper Egypt are united under one ruler (Menes)	c3100bc
The building of the pyramids	2650–2400
The period of the Old Kingdom	2649–2150
The Middle Kingdom	2134–1783
The New Kingdom (Tuthmosis, Hatshepsut, Akenaten, Tutankhamun, Rameses I–III)	1550–1070
The battle of Kadesh (Rameses II claims victory over the Hittites)	1285
Nubians occupy part of Egypt	724
The Persians invade (Darius, Xerxes, Artaxerxes)	525
Alexander the Great conquers Egypt and drives out the Persians (Ptolemy I)	332
Battle of Actium against the Romans (death of Cleopatra)	31
The Romans invade (Egypt is added to their Empire)	30

Why do we need to know about the Ancient Egyptians?

Ancient Egypt was one of the world's earliest civilizations, and as such it provides important clues about how the civilized world developed. Basic skills were developed in Ancient Egypt such as house building and farming. Ancient Egypt was the world's richest and most sophisticated ancient civilization. It built the world's largest ancient buildings, the pyramids, and developed one of the world's earliest writing systems.

At Key Stage 2, Ancient Egypt is the most popular world history option in the Curriculum, partly because it is more accessible to teachers and children than the other choices.

How do we know about the Ancient Egyptians?

At about the same time that Menes was uniting Egypt, the picture writing known as hieroglyphic text was invented. Historians therefore have evidence of these people, written on papyrus and stone. They also have the written evidence, eyewitness accounts and judgements of literate people who came into close contact with the Ancient Egyptians in later times, particularly the Greeks and Romans. Egypt is also mentioned in the Old Testament of the Bible (see the book of Genesis and the story of Joseph).

Huge structures (the temple at Abu Simbel and the pyramids at Giza for example), the contents of tombs, and the preserved bodies of the Ancient Egyptians themselves all provide a great deal of interesting detail about Ancient Egypt. We have furniture, games, paintings, jewellery, pottery, books and even textiles to study.

What happened to the Ancient Egyptians?

The Ancient Egyptian civilization lasted for over 3000 years, and even survived the interruption of foreign rule by a number of conquerors: Ethiopians (Nubians), Greeks and Romans. But on the death of Queen Cleopatra in 31BC, the Romans took over. There were no more pharaohs and native rule ended. Egypt became part of a wider Mediterranean culture centred on Rome, but some cultural practices lingered on, and we know that the practice of mummification was not finally abandoned until some time in the 4th century AD. A 7th century invasion by Arabs made Egypt the predominantly Muslim country it is today.

Of their spoken language, which must have existed for thousands of years, very little remains. It is thought that the liturgy of the Coptic Christians has its root in ancient Egyptian, but we have no other legacy of their speech.

Hittites – powerful enemies of the Egyptians around 1650BC, their empire centered on modern Turkey and Syria.

Nubians – came from southern Egypt and northern Sudan, an area that became Egyptianized, although Nubians did dominate Egypt in the 8th century BC.

Irrigation – the provision of water, by the use of artificial canals, to land lacking in moisture in order to grow crops.

Rosetta Stone – this provided the key which enabled scholars to read hieroglyphs. It was discovered at Rashid (Rosetta) in the Nile delta in AD1799. The inscription on the stone was in hieroglyphs, demotic script and Greek. It still took over 20 years to decipher it – an achievement credited to Jean Champollion in 1822.

Cartouche – groups of hieroglyphs contained within an oval shape, indicating a royal or divine name.

Papyrus – a fleshy plant that used to grow in dense thickets in the Nile marshes. Thin strips were cut from the stem of the reed and laid side by side on flat stones. A second layer was laid at right angles on top. After being beaten with wooden mallets, a surface for writing on was produced.

Shabti – also Ushabti; models of workers that were buried with mummies and who would spring to life on the command of Osiris to do the work required of the mummified person on their journey through the afterlife.

Book of the Dead – the journey of the spirit in the afterlife was recorded on papyrus known as the 'Book of the Dead'. The journey showed the blissful world of the Egyptian heaven, a land like the Nile, rich in wildlife and food. The Egyptians called it 'The Book of the Coming into Day'.

Natron – a whitish, yellow mineral that occurs in salt lakes. Used to dry out fluids in corpses undergoing mummification.

Luxor – the home town of the kings of the New Kingdom from around 1550BC onwards. They built their palaces here and chose to be buried in the rock-cut tombs of the Valley of the Kings (sometimes referred to as Thebes).

Kadesh – site in northern Syria of the great battle between Rameses II and the Hittites. Rameses claimed the victory although it was indecisive. The Arabic is *Qadesh* but Kadesh is acceptable and easier to pronounce.

Pharaoh – Rulers or kings of Egypt. Pharaohs were so called because they lived in a palace called a great house or *'per-ao'*, hence the derivation.

Nilometer – a graduated stone used to measure flood levels.

Egyptian society

Farming

The rhythm of Egyptian life was dictated by the Nile and its annual inundation. Between July and October, rains in central Sudan and Ethiopia raised the level of the river and caused it to flood, fertilizing the land with a layer of silt. After the flood, the land was ploughed and crops sown. Tomb models have revealed that seeds were scattered by hand and farmers used oxen to draw their ploughs and trample them in by livestock. Emmer wheat and barley (never corn) were sown – there were usually two successive crops harvested in April or May. Men gathered in the harvest while the women were responsible for winnowing the grain. They did this by tossing it in the air so the light stalks blew away and the heavy seeds fell to the ground. In Roman times the Egyptians were forced to grow more wheat and produce three harvests each year in order to feed Rome. Flax was the other main crop (this was used for linen, matting and rope), although vegetables, fruits and vines were cultivated in smaller plots.

From the river itself, and the marshy delta areas, the Egyptians harvested fish and fowl, as well as papyrus and reeds for making papyrus scrolls, baskets and other domestic materials.

Artisans

From accounts and records we know that the Egyptians were skilled artists and workmen. They worked in stone, metal and wood, and produced fine objects in pottery, glass, precious metal and stone. All craftsmen served an apprenticeship, and virtually all worked directly or indirectly for the royal, government or temple workshops.

Writing

The Ancient Egyptians developed a system of writing called hieroglyphics that used pictures and signs which represented sounds, not words. Egyptian kings had their own hieroglyphs representing their name, known as cartouches (see opposite). How a word was pronounced would decide which hieroglyph would be used. Although the language has been deciphered we still have no clues as to how it was pronounced. The Ancient Egyptian alphabet comprised 24 basic signs that could be written from left to right, right to left, or from top to bottom.

Houses

As always there was a difference between rich and poor homes. Houses of the poor were made with sun-baked mud bricks; houses of the wealthy were made of stone. The Egyptians mastered the art of working in stone at an early date: all the more permanent buildings were built of stone.

In general, houses were built on a square plan around a living room and had a flat roof. Their exteriors were whitewashed and the walls and floors inside could be painted, plastered or tiled. Larger, wealthier houses had bathrooms that consisted of a stone slab, which was stood on while washing, and there would have been an earth-closet toilet. For these ablutions poorer people used pots and bowls, which would be emptied some distance from the house. In larger urban areas, town houses could be two or three storeys and had high windows without glass.

It seems that many homes had some fitted furniture. Low platforms on which to sit or make up a bed were common. Wooden chests were used for storage and besides the usual chairs and tables, extra comfort was provided by wall hangings, mats and cushions. All homes had places for statues of household gods.

The main meal of the day was taken in the evening, and was a family affair. Cooking was done over an open fire or in a pottery oven fuelled by straw, wood, leaves and animal dung. Bread, vegetables and fruits formed the basis of the Egyptian diet, and food was flavoured with garlic, herbs and spices, and sweetened using honey and dates. Wealthy Egyptians ate meat and fish mainly on special occasions. Beer made from barley was the most common drink (written records mention 17 varieties), although wine, milk and water were also drunk.

Leisure

Of course the Egyptians found some time to enjoy themselves, although most activities ended at dark when everyone went to bed. We know that children had simple toys and games such as spinning tops, balls, dolls and wooden animals, and adults took part in sports, dancing and making music. There were also several types of board game that they could play. The wealthy upper classes had more time for leisure and would entertain each other at banquets or go on hunting or fishing expeditions into the marshes or desert.

Warfare
The overwhelming impression one gets of life in Ancient Egypt is that of a peaceful agricultural existence, yet warfare interrupted the peace of the Nile Valley when powerful invaders sought to take the wealth of the Egyptians for themselves. But during the period of the New Kingdom, especially under Rameses III (AD1182–1151), the Egyptians were a powerful nation and made military forays into Palestine and beyond.

At the heart of the army were the infantry who were armed with spears, shields and battleaxes. Rameses also used archers, mounted in horse-drawn chariots, to rain arrows down upon the enemy. The chariots were big enough to carry three men, and were drawn by two horses. The arrows had an estimated range of 200 metres (650 feet). The army was well-organized, with different ranks of officers in charge of specific groups of men. Campaigns were fought in Nubia, Palestine and as far away as Syria.

Probably the most famous battle in Egyptian history is the battle of Kadesh, largely because it is so well-recorded in sculptured reliefs. It was fought by Rameses II against the ancient enemies, the Hittites. In 1285 Rameses stood with his army before the fortress of Kadesh in northern Syria. The Hittites, hidden behind the fortress, ambushed Rameses who stood his ground with some 2500 chariots. At the last, victory (or at least a draw) at the battle of Kadesh was snatched from defeat by the arrival of reinforcements who attacked the Hittites from the rear.

The Egyptians had various enemies at different times. They were conquered by the Greeks under Alexander the Great (see Chapter 4, page 46), by the Romans (see Chapter 5, page 66) and by the Persians. They fought against the Hittites, the Nubians and the Sea Peoples of the Mediterranean.

Why you need to know these facts	Children need to understand how events shaped the lives of people in the past, and that such changes took place within the period when the Ancient Egyptian civilization flourished.

● We have no evidence of any Ancient Egyptian woman who learned to read or write.

● Papyrus does not grow anywhere naturally in Egypt today. The tourist trade in papyrus is largely met by using 'paper' made with banana skins.

● Animals were often part of Egyptian households, and cats in particular were highly revered. When a pet cat died the whole family would shave off their eyebrows as a sign that they were in mourning.

● Wall and tomb paintings have revealed what the Ancient Egyptians wore. The most common material was white linen made from flax, which the men wore as loincloths and the women as long dresses. Leather or reed sandals were worn on their feet. Children wore few clothes, and in many paintings are shown naked with their heads shaved, leaving one or two long locks of hair called 'locks of youth'.

There were few trees in Egypt, so all timber had to come from the Lebanon.
In fact there were (and are) many trees in Egypt. Pollen analysis by archaeologists has shown that all types of trees existed in Egypt (hardwood, softwood, deciduous and coniferous) and that it always had lots of native wood.

The Egyptians spoke hieroglyphics.
Hieroglyphs were written symbols, but the spoken language was Ancient Egyptian. Nobody knows what it sounded like, although Coptic, surviving only in the liturgical language of the Coptic Church, has its roots in Ancient Egyptian.

● Get the children to design a picture strip cartoon showing a day in the life of an Egyptian farmer.

● Children could design a cartouche of their name.

● Get the children to write an account of a hunting trip – undertaking some research first. It could be into the marshes, or perhaps the desert.

● Read a story from the Old Testament about the Egyptians, such as 'Joseph and his coat of many colours'.

● Conduct a class discussion about life in Ancient Egypt. One group should argue in favour of life in those times, while another points out the disadvantages.

● The children could copy the Egyptian style of painting. They could depict themselves and their family and pets or an important event from their lives.

Beliefs, burial and the afterlife

Gods

The pattern of Egyptian belief was very different from the Romans or Greeks and is quite complicated. You can divide Egyptian gods into four groups:

● First there were the gods of the cosmos – the stars and heaven – that were included in Ancient Egyptian mythology but were not worshipped.

● Then there were 'domestic' deities, which equated closely to modern superstitions – amulets that protected or brought good luck. Also not part of any system of worship.

● Next there were the gods of the dead (shown below). These judged people's actions in life and ruled the 'Duat', or underworld. These were only worshipped towards the end of the Ancient Egyptian period, when Egypt was strongly under the influence of Greece and Rome.

● Finally there were the local, and most important, gods. These were worshipped because they were believed to bring benefit to their local place. The local god (simply referred to as 'god' in most cases) was the only one of any relevance in the lives of the people, so the Egyptians were, in a sense, monotheistic. Souls of the ancient dead of a place formed these gods because they were thought to be benevolent towards their own locality. Worship, in the form of offerings three times a day, was really a kind of deal, an act of barter. It was not about prayer or praise; if a god failed to deliver he might be cursed, a broken promise written on a pot and then smashed against a wall.

ANUBIS   HORUS   OSIRIS

The Egyptians never worshipped animals or thought of their gods as having animal heads. When animal-headed gods were portrayed on temple walls, this was to explain to illiterate people the characteristic of the god (a kind of visual metaphor), and the pictures were used rather as wall paintings on the walls of medieval churches were used.

If you wanted to make a special request to a god, it was thought that they would take more notice of one of their creatures than of the plea of a mere mortal. So creatures were bred in the temple for sale, slaughter and mummification. Placed in a pot, their souls were thought to fly straight to the god with the person's request.

The journey to heaven

If you wanted to live forever in the company of Osiris, King of the Dead, in a pleasant land (like Egypt) with rich harvests of grain (but no work to do), you had to make a journey through the underworld. At the end of the journey, and before you could qualify for eternal life, your heart was weighed by the god Anubis against the feather of truth. This was to see how well you had behaved on Earth. If it weighed too much, there was a monster called Ammit ('devourer of the dead') ready to eat it. The journey was a kind of obstacle course, with a crocodile to avoid as well as an incredible serpent, a fierce fire, and a monkey with a trap. To make this journey easier, a collection of around 200 magic spells was written called the 'Book of the Dead'. Copies of these sheets of papyrus were placed in tombs or between the layers of bandages of a mummy, near the legs.

ISIS THOTH BASTET

The Egyptian heaven was perceived as part of two earths that ran in parallel. The Ancient Egyptians lived in the top one and the afterlife was below. The sun travelled across their sky, then set to travel across the sky of the afterlife, before returning at dawn.

Mummies

The Egyptians loved living and were not obsessed with death. They saw death as an extension of life, which was good. They expected all the good things to continue after they died. However, for the journey to the afterlife to be negotiated successfully it was best, so they thought, that the body was preserved; if the body was destroyed the spirit might be lost. So those people of wealth or status, such as pharaohs and the nobility, had their bodies mummified by priests.

The word 'mummy' comes from an Arabic word for bitumen (mummified bodies are black in appearance) and has nothing to do with parenthood. We know how the process worked from x-ray and other examinations of the bodies, but chiefly from the writings of the Greek, Herodotus, who wrote a description of the process, which he observed on his travels around Egypt in 450BC.

It took the priests 70 days to mummify a body. The liver, lungs, stomach and intestines were removed and placed in special 'canopic' jars. Only the heart was left in place, as this was felt to be essential for the journey to the afterlife. It was a lengthy, delicate, messy and smelly process. The brain was removed through the nostrils by a hook. All the moisture had to be removed to ensure preservation, and this was done by washing the body in palm wine and then covering it in natron, a naturally occurring salt. After 40 days, the embalmers would rub the skin with oils and pack the body with spices, linen, sawdust and sand to reshape it. Finally, they would wrap it in layers of bandages soaked in resin. Magic spells and amulets were often folded into the layers to bring good luck in the afterlife. Then the mummy was sealed in its case.

The process was finished off before entombment with ceremonies and prayers. A collection of useful artefacts for the afterlife, such as prayers, food, shabti and furniture was placed with the mummy. Shabti were pottery figures representing the servants who would carry out the agricultural duties that would be demanded of the deceased, so they were very important objects in the tomb. The tombs of the great pharaohs have yielded incredible treasures of great value, but the wealth buried with the

pharaohs was a considerable temptation to thieves and
most tombs that we know of were robbed at some time.
Only a fraction of what was buried has survived to
modern times.

Pyramids

For about 100 years pharaohs were buried in pyramids, but
because of their size they could not be hidden, so the tombs
were easily robbed. We know of 88 pyramids, and all but
two are bare inside. Clever though they were in their
construction, sometimes with false doors, tunnels and dead
ends, thieves always managed to get in eventually, because
the prize was so great and the temptation irresistible.

Then, in about 1500BC, the idea developed of hiding the
tomb as well as the treasure. For the next 500 years
pharaohs cut into the stone floor and wall of a secret valley
to the west of Luxor to create their burial places. This
valley, known as the 'Valley of the Kings', is surrounded
by high cliffs. It is hidden away from the Nile on its
western side.

These hidden tombs have wonderfully decorated walls,
replete with paintings of kings. Although some were
robbed, others, such as the tomb of Tutankhamun, have
been found virtually in tact. Perhaps some have yet to be
found and hold their secrets still.

Building the pyramids

Large numbers of people were needed to build the
pyramids. At Giza, archaeologists have found homes for
8000 people, which are thought to be those of the workers
who built the pyramids. The stone was cut in quarries and
moved by boat crews of 60 divided into four groups of 15
men. Each group had a daily quota of stone to move (a
quota that was never met!)

Giza is particularly notable for its pyramids because
there, on the edge of the desert, 9 kilometres (6 miles) from
Cairo, stands the largest of all – the Great Pyramid. It is the
last surviving of the seven wonders of the ancient world. It
was built around 2550BC, and was built from limestone and
was faced with finer limestone from across the Nile at Tura.
The workers used ropes attached to smooth wooden rollers
coated in fine mud to help haul the massive blocks of stone
across the desert. Each block of stone, put in place by hand,
weighed 25 000 kilograms – about the weight of an adult
male hippopotamus. There were 2 300 000 such blocks. The
Great Pyramid stood 146.6 metres (481 feet) high originally,
and the error of alignment of the base is only half a degree

at the maximum. It was a tomb for King Cheops (the
Egyptians call him Khufu).

Subject facts

Mummies, pyramids and the tombs of pharaohs provide us
with some of our most significant evidence about the
Ancient Egyptians. The pyramids are also worthy of study in
their own right, as one of the ancient wonders of the world.

Amazing facts

● Some people believe in the curse of the pyramids. After
Howard Carter excavated the tomb of Tutankhamun in
1922, this belief became very popular. Although Lord
Cannar died shortly after the excavation of an infected
mosquito bite, both Howard Carter and the young boy
who was the first to enter the burial chamber lived well into
old age.
● Experiments by Japanese Egyptologists have shown that,
by using a ramp of 12 degrees – as given on mathematical
papyri – a block of stone weighing 25 000kg could be
dragged on a sledge by eight men with little difficulty, but
we do not know precisely how the pyramids and obelisks
were built.

**Common
misconceptions**

That there were slaves in ancient Egypt.
If we define a slave as a person with no identity or rights
before the law, then these did not exist. Every person –
male, female, foreigner or native – had equal rights under
the law. Even prisoners in battle, although handed out as
rewards to brave soldiers, still had rights. However,
everyone was a servant (all worked directly or indirectly for
the state). Pharaoh himself was referred to as 'god's
servant'. The emotive term slave – a person with no rights –
cannot be applied until Roman times when the Romans
enslaved the Egyptians.

Teaching ideas

● Using clay for the base, get the children to make a papier
mâché replica of the mask of Tutankhamun.
● Tell the children, 'You are pharaoh – prepare to meet thy
tomb'. Get the children to make an inventory of all the
objects they would like to be buried with when they die.
● Some say that disturbing the graves of people buried long
ago is wrong. Have a class debate about this.

● The pyramids were ancient monuments even in the time of the later Egyptians. Get the children to describe a day out to the pyramids as if they were a child being taken by his father to visit them 2500 years ago.

● As a class, build a scale model of the Great Pyramid at Giza. Check all the measurements first. Can the children work out the mathematical net of a pyramid?

● Make a wall display about the seven wonders of the ancient world.

● Investigate Anubis, Horus, Re, Thoth and Sakhmet. How many other Egyptian gods can the children find out about?

Important people and places

The land

Subject facts

The most powerful people in Ancient Egypt were the pharaohs who were kings of Egypt and who ruled as absolute monarchs. The source of their power was land – all land belonged to the pharaohs. If they gave land to anyone it was actually only the produce of the land that was given and not the land itself, and even this produce could be taxed. At the time, 98 per cent of people worked on the land, so ownership of land equalled power.

The rich Nile valley was the most important place to the Egyptians – they called it the 'Black Land', because each year when the Nile was in flood, thick, dark mud was washed over the banks. This soil alongside the river was very fertile and was used to grow crops. To the east and west lay the deserts, and these were referred to as the 'Red Land'. Here there was nothing but vast stony wastes where rain was scarce and nothing grew.

The great pharaohs

Hatshepsut 1498–1483BC (All early dates are approximate)
Hatshepsut married her half-brother Tuthmosis II, and when he died she should not have become pharaoh, as succession was through the male line. But nevertheless she took over government for her five-year-old stepson Tuthmosis III, for whom she was supposed to be acting as regent. Hers was a peaceful and culturally rich reign – she seems to have been a woman of considerable strength of character (she is often portrayed as male), and held on to government for about 20 years until her death.

Akhenaten 1350–1334BC

He introduced many changes to the lives of his people, not
least of which was to abandon the old religion with its many
gods. Akenaten was a monotheist – that is, he believed that
there was only one god: Aten the sun god. The old temples
in the area of Tel el Amarna were closed down and
Akhenaten built a new capital, 300 kilometres (186 miles)
down the Nile from the old city of Thebes. The new capital
was also called Akhenaten and was dedicated to the sun
god. But there is no evidence that Akhenaten imposed
monotheism on his people, nor that he worshipped the sun
as God – rather he used the sun as a metaphor for God.
Some people moved north to set up new homes there, but
the new capital only lasted for about 15 years, and after
Akhenaten's death they moved back to their old homes and
returned to the old religion again.

Nefertiti 14th century BC (ruled with Akhenaten above)

Half-sister of Tutankhamun, she was married to Akhenaten,
and appears to have been a powerful influence, especially
in encouraging monotheism: she effectively ruled with
him. Their successors took exception to their disparaging of
the old gods and tried to obliterate their memory by
removing their names from inscriptions and pulling down
their temples.

Tutankhamun 1334–1325BC

A boy ruler – he was only nine when he came to the throne
– who achieved immortality largely because of the
discovery of his tomb and extensive grave goods. The tomb
was found in 1922 and entered in February 1923 by Howard
Carter. Tutankhamun's tomb had been robbed (the
footprints of the robbers were found), but the robbers were
probably caught in the act and most of the tomb seemed
intact. His famous gold-masked coffin was encased in two
other coffins.

Rameses II (The Great) 1279–1212BC

His victory over arch-enemies the Hittites in the battle of
Kadesh (in Syria) is recorded on many reliefs, although it
was not as decisive as the celebratory sculptures might
suggest. Rameses built the huge temple at Abu Simbel and
more statues than any other pharaoh. He ruled for 67 years.

Ptolemy Soter 323–285BC

Alexander the Great's general, and possibly the greatest of
them, became ruler of Egypt when Alexander died in 323BC.

Ptolemy ruled Egypt from Alexandria. He founded a Greek-speaking dynasty that ruled for 300 years in the same way as traditional Egyptian rulers. Ptolemy spent much of his reign defending the frontiers of his land, and earned himself the title *Soter*, which means saviour. He abdicated in 285BC in favour of his son. He died in 283BC.

Cleopatra 69–30BC

Cleopatra was the last Greek pharaoh (the last of the Ptolemy dynasty). She lost her throne in a palace coup, but was restored to power by Julius Caesar. She formed a political and personal alliance with Marc Antony by whom she bore three children. Marc Antony was apparently completely besotted with Cleopatra and left his wife and children for her, but ambition brought them into conflict with Rome and Marc Antony's infatuation lost him public respect and support. They were defeated by the Romans under Augustus at the battle of Actium in 31BC. After her lover Antony had died in her arms, she killed herself by taking poison, possibly by causing a snake to bite her breast.

Why you need to know these facts

History is primarily about people, and the most significant people in Ancient Egypt, about whom substantial evidence exists, are the pharaohs. To understand the Ancient Egyptians, we must learn about pharaohs.

Amazing facts

● There must have been a great deal of consent in the exercise of power by the pharaohs because there are few records of assassinations, and when assassination did happen it was usually to dispose of a usurper.

Common misconceptions

Cleopatra was beautiful.
This idea dates from Tudor times. Her contemporaries thought she was plump and plain but that she had great charm, wit and intelligence.

The Ancient Egyptians looked like white Europeans.
This was clearly not so. The Nubians from the south formed part of Egypt at one time, and they were African. Painted

limestone statues of government officials show men having darker skin than women. This was normal practice: women were expected to have less exposure to the sun and thus were always depicted with paler skins in murals.

● On an outline map of the eastern Mediterranean, mark all the places of significance in the history of Ancient Egypt.
● Design a travel poster advertising the tourist sites worth visiting in modern Egypt.
● Choose a famous Egyptian pharaoh and write an obituary for him or her listing all their achievements.
● Study the geography of the River Nile, then write an encyclopaedia entry giving as much data as possible. Look at climate, land use and physical geography.
● Pretend that the Egyptian 'style' has become fashionable. Design a range of goods (clothes, furniture, objects) for sale in a well-known shop.
● Imagine you are in jail. You were a tomb robber caught in the act. Describe the events of the ill-fated robbery.

Resources

First-hand experience of the evidence is much less accessible for this topic than for others. However, there are a great number of artefacts in British museums, not only in the British Museum itself, which of course has many including the Rosetta Stone and many mummies. In the 19th and 20th centuries many European archaeologists removed material from ancient sites and brought it back to European museums which is why, if you cannot go to Egypt you will find that much of it has come to you.

Books
Egypt is a popular topic; consequently there are many reference books for children, although there are variations in the quality of scholarship so don't be surprised if children find differences between books. Material produced by the British Museum is very reliable, see *The Collections of the British Museum* by Sir D Wilson (British Museum Publications) for an illustrated summary of the collection.

Here are a few useful children's books:
Egypt by Jane Shuter (Wayland) – recent, well-produced and detailed.
Egyptian Town by S Steedman and D Antram (Franklin

Watts) – detailed views from a bird's eye, different.
Valley of the Kings by R Alcraft (Heinemann) – a kind of
tourist's history, fine original photographs.
The Egyptians by G Chapman (Heinemann) – craft ideas of
variable quality but it could contain just what you are
looking for.
Pharaohs and Mummies by Anita Ganeri (Penguin).
Ancient Egypt by G Hart (Eyewitness Guide, Dorling
Kindersley) – the well-tested DK formula works particularly
well for this topic, packed with information that can be
accessed on a number of levels.

Practical ideas, pictures and material for children to
work with can be found in:
Eyewitness Project Pack, Mummy (Dorling Kindersley).
Resource Pack, Ancient Egypt by P Noble (Collins).
The Ancient Egyptians Activity Book by L Manniche (British
Museum Press).
Egyptian Life postcard pack (British Museum Publications).
Life in Ancient Egypt (British Museum Publications) –
through the eyes of a young girl, teacher's notes and video.
Egypt, Video Plus (BBC Educational Publications) – a series
of useful programmes on video.

Further reading for teachers:
An Introduction to Ancient Egypt by TGH James (British
Museum Publications).
Life in Ancient Egypt by A Erman (Dover).

Contacts
A key contact address is British Museum Education Service,
Great Russell Street, London WC1B (tel: 020 7636 1555;
www.thebritishmuseum.ac.uk).
A major and little-visited collection can be seen in:
Petrie Museum of Egyptian Archaeology, University College,
Gower Street, London WC1E 6BT (tel: 020 7679 2884).
The Smithsonian Institute has a good website with excellent
material (www.si.edu).

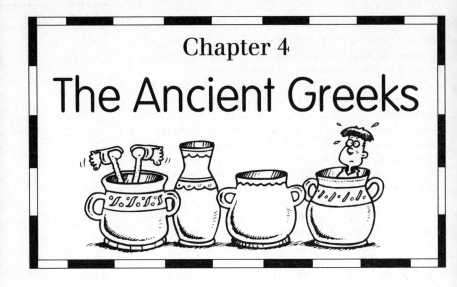

Chapter 4
The Ancient Greeks

Today the Olympic Games is probably the only festival that is truly world-wide, and yet it is just one small legacy of a people who gave us not only the essentials of democracy and modern civilization, but also the very words to describe them. For us, the story of the Ancient Greeks begins around 800 years before the birth of Christ, when the names of winners at the Olympic Games were first written down. Before that moment, we have only the silent and sketchy evidence of archaeology to bear witness to the world of the Ancient Greeks.

Introducing the Ancient Greeks

Subject facts

Who were the Ancient Greeks?

The Greek civilization developed mainly in small city-states (see page 59), and predominantly in the states of Athens and Sparta. The Ancient Greek city-states had frequent quarrels and violent disputes with each other, and were never united as a single nation. However, the people were bound by a common language, religion and culture. The Greeks called themselves *Hellenes* and their country *Hellas*. Their civilization reached its height in Athens in the 4th and

5th centuries BC. It was during this period that the Greeks produced their great literature and architecture, and developed world-changing ideas such as democracy.

With numerous islands and deep fjords, Greece covers only 80 650km², yet the Greeks colonized land from southern Russia to Libya and from Spain to Turkey and Syria. Under the leadership of Alexander the Great, Greek culture spread to what is now West Pakistan.

So Classical Greece is particularly hard to pin down to one place, and some historians have even suggested that it should be regarded as an idea rather than a physical entity – it tended to be wherever Greek was spoken.

With the conquests of Alexander the Great, the Greek world expanded and moved its centre eastwards in what is known as the Hellenistic period (323–146BC).

Timeline - (The dates for these ancient times are approximate.)

First written record of the Olympic Games.	776BC (traditionally)
First triremes (galleys powered by oarsmen in units of three) built – Greek warships that dominated the Mediterranean well into Roman times.	700
The use of metal coins spread from modern Turkey to being used all over the Greek world. Beginning of the city-states and the expansion of the Greek world.	7th century BC
Reforms of Solon – beginning of democracy in Athens.	594
First drama festival held in Athens.	534
Clisthenes reorganized the government of Athens so that full power lay with the Citizen Assembly. He called the system one of equal rights (isonomia), but created what was essentially the first democracy. The word democracy *(rule of the people) came in to general use in the 5th century BC.*	508
Wars against the Persian Empire.	492–449
Battle of Marathon. The marathon race was introduced to the Olympic Games after a soldier had run over 42 kilometres (26 miles) from Marathon to Athens to inform the city of a victory over the Persians. He dropped dead on arrival.	490
Battle of Salamis. Greek victory over a Persian fleet which outnumbered them by three to one.	480
Battle of Thermopylae. The Spartans under King Leonidas held the pass against the invading Persians. The Greeks were betrayed and outflanked; Leonidas sent away most of his army before they became trapped and stayed with 300 men to hold off the Persians. They were all killed. Xerxes nailed Leonidas' body to a cross.	431–404
Peloponnesian War between Sparta and Athens and their allies.	359

338	*Philip of Macedon (Alexander the Great's father) comes to power and begins his domination of the Greek world.*
331	*Philip defeats the Athenians and their allies and gains mastery over Greece.*
327	*Alexander defeats Darius III at the battle of Gaugamela. End of the Persian Empire.*
23	*Alexander enters India via the Khyber Pass.*
	Death of Alexander the Great in Babylon.
	In the 300 years to the death of Cleopatra in 30BC, the Greek civilization spread across the known world, but political independence ended. Dominance of the world passed to the Romans.

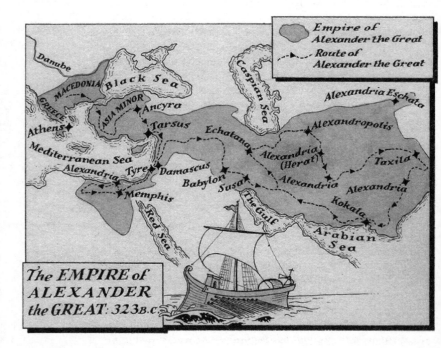

The EMPIRE of ALEXANDER the GREAT: 323B.C.

Why do we need to know about the Ancient Greeks?

Almost every part of western European culture owes some debt to the Greeks. From sport and medicine to politics and architecture, from drama and literature to philosophy and mathematics, the influence of the Ancient Greeks has been fundamental and can still be felt today. For this reason Ancient Greece is part of the Programme of Study for Key Stage 2 history in the National Curriculum. Junior-age children have to learn about the achievements, the way of life and the legacy of the Ancient Greek civilization.

How do we know about the Ancient Greeks?

In the Classical period the Greeks had a fully developed alphabet, so therefore their voices can speak to us across the ages through the written word. The records of Greek traders, writers, politicians and poets give us insights into their intellectual as well as their physical lives. We need to be wary though – all our information about Sparta comes largely from Athenian writers because the Spartans did not write histories or other books.

Archaeology, coupled with ever-improving scientific techniques, provides a mass of evidence, not only through the tools, weapons and artefacts unearthed, but also through the skilful interpretation and re-interpretation of the sites where they were found.

Myth, legend and both oral and written traditions are also valuable to the historian and yield further insights.

Not only have we the fine architecture to remind us of their skill, but also jewellery, artefacts and many vases which yield useful evidence about society and what the Ancient Greeks actually looked like.

What happened to the Ancient Greeks?

After the death of Alexander in 323BC, Greek ideas and civilization continued to spread, but their political independence ended and the Romans became rulers of the world. However, many ideas and aspects of the Western way of life today have their roots in Ancient Greece.

What is the legacy of the Ancient Greeks?

The influence of Greek culture on Western society today is greater than that of any other nation in history. Many banks, town halls and prestigious buildings exhibit columns and pediments taken directly from Greek designs, and there is hardly an area of intellectual activity – literature, science, aesthetics, politics or philosophy – on which Greek ideas have not had a fundamental impact:

- The Greeks invented the literary forms of epic poetry and drama. Aeschylus, Sophocles and Euripides were great tragic playwrights of the 5th century BC, and Aristophanes was a memorable comic poet and dramatist.
- Herodotus is called 'the father of history' because he was the first to reconstruct the past using documentary records rather than relying on myths and legends. He wrote a history of the Persian Wars. Thucydides wrote a history of the Peloponnesian Wars in which he was an eyewitness, but he also discussed causes and sought to draw general conclusions about events.
- Philosophy originated in Ancient Greece and was raised to an art form in the dialogues of Plato, who was a pupil of Socrates. Socrates died without ever writing a word (his beliefs are known through the writings of his pupils Plato and Xenophon), but he turned philosophy into discussions about the nature of man, morals and the universe. Aristotle followed Plato and was a considerable influence on the thinkers of the Middle Ages. He also initiated biological studies based upon the collection of data. The philosophers (or stoics) of the Hellenistic period focused on virtue and living according to Divine Will, and clearly affected the way in which Christianity developed.
- On the island of Cos, the Hippocratic School of Physicians invented medicine as a scientific art. Archimedes calculated the value of pi; Aristarchus worked out that the Sun was larger than the Earth and that the planets revolved around the Sun; Eratosthenes calculated the circumference of the Earth to within a margin of 322 kilometres (200 miles). The Greeks used mechanical devices such as the screw and the cogwheel and even used steam power and air pressure.
- In art and architecture they made revolutionary strides and produced the West's first naturalist sculpture and painting. Their architecture, with its columns and classical orders, had an influence that endures still.
- The notion that every citizen was a potential politician, and that the business of government was therefore of interest to everyone, was a Greek one. The Greeks effectively invented not only democracy (usually dated from the reforms of Solon in Athens *c*573BC) but politics itself. Plato and Aristotle developed political theory and the concept of the ideal state.
- Perhaps more tangible legacies, from the children's point of view, are to be found in the words we use. Suffixes and prefixes such as -ology, -phobia, tech-, geo-, photo-; names like Alexander, Helen, Nike and Mars, and words such as stadium and dinosaur are all within the child's experience.

The children will also have heard Greek myths and legends and, of course, be familiar with the Olympic Games.
● The Greeks were responsible for our alphabet's evolution into a flexible and powerful tool and for passing it on to the Romans.

Vocabulary

Acropolis – centrally located, well-defended area of a Greek town containing the main religious and civic buildings.
City-state – a unit of government and settlement (*polis* in Greek). Athens, Sparta and Thebes are examples.
Hoplite – a heavily armed infantryman.
Parthenon – a temple in the Athenian Acropolis built in the 5th century BC.
Some modern words have a root meaning that is from Ancient Greek, for example:
Aristocracy – rule of the best born.
Democracy – rule of the people.
Geometry – to measure the land.
Machine – a device.
Philosophy – love of wisdom.
Physics – nature.
Politics – from 'citizen' (*polis* = city).

Ancient Greek society

Life was simple by modern standards: it was hard, short and often brutal. We would probably regard the Greek way of life as primitive, yet it still had intellectual power and vitality that astonishes us even today.

Subject facts

Architecture

When we think of Ancient Greece we often think first of great stone buildings such as the Parthenon with their grand columns. The Parthenon was built on the Acropolis in Athens as a shrine to the goddess Athena, and no expense was spared in its construction. Within the Parthenon the Athenians erected a statue to Athena carved by Pheidias, an acclaimed sculptor. It towered 11 metres (36 feet) high and was richly decorated with gold and ivory. The Parthenon was finished in 432BC after 15 years of work. The columns supporting the roof were in the Doric style (tapering fluted columns and round undecorated capitals) commonly used on mainland Greece. The Ionic style had slender columns and scroll capitals, and was used in the Greek cities in Turkey. Both styles were in use in the 5th century. The Corinthian style (highly decorated capitals, used greatly by the Romans) came in to use at the end of the century.

Houses

It is difficult to get a clear picture of Greek houses because they were largely made of sun-dried brick laid on stone foundations, and have not survived. They appear to have been quite simple structures, roofed with terracotta tiles, with separate areas for women and children. Town houses were probably more grand with a greater number of rooms.

Life expectancy

Everyone had to work to live and there were not too many surpluses to support the old, the sick or the weak – your family was your only lifeline. Life expectancy for men was around 35 years. Women, because of the risks of childbirth, could not expect to live so long. Death rates among babies were extremely high. Slaves, particularly those working in the Athenian silver mines, had a short life expectancy.

Slaves

Quality of life depended then, as now, on who you were. Slaves were at the bottom of the social ladder and were not only captives of war but could also be debtors sold into slavery in payment for money owed; this was sometimes used as a quick way of raising capital. Solon, credited with the founding of democracy brought in, as part of his famous reforms, a law cancelling agricultural debts and emancipated all Athenians sold into slavery. Slaves had a pretty poor existence, although some lived as well as poorer citizens in the cities. At one point there were more than 20 000 slaves in Athens and its silver mines – death came early if you worked in the mines. Some slaves were Greek, but most came from barbarian tribes. The police of Athens were Scythian archers – state slaves bought in south Russia.

In their own words

> *Slaves and the lower classes are treated very freely here. No one beats a slave or expects him to stand aside in the street to let him pass. Athenians dress no better than slaves, so if there was a law saying that you could beat a slave one would often beat a citizen by mistake.*
> Pseudo-Xenophon I, 5th century BC

Women

Women were the largest underclass: they were ignored politically and many hardly ever left the home. Girls would be married off at 13 or 14 years of age as result of financial or political deals arranged by men, and the bride was excluded from the celebration. Wives could be beaten, even killed with impunity. Legally they had few rights but they did hold important domestic power in richer houses, supervising the household and its complement of slaves. Their social position varied, and Sappho and the women of Lesbos seem to have enjoyed greater freedom than other Greek women (Sappho's poetry is still admired today). Women and slaves were expected to wait on men when they held drinking parties called symposia. Female slaves then danced while the respectable women withdrew.

Food

Diet again depended upon wealth, but bread and porridge were staple foods. Fruit and vegetables were eaten in large quantities when in season (apples, pears, pomegranates and figs) but meat was largely reserved for special occasions. Fish was a popular food, especially in towns near the sea. Hunting and fishing were important pastimes as Greek soil is mainly poor and a great deal of effort was required to provide a useful crop. Wine was everybody's drink and both rich and poor consumed large quantities, usually diluted with water.

Clothes

Vase pictures in particular give us a very good idea about what the normal citizen wore. Bearing in mind the hot climate of Greece, it comes as no surprise that both men and women wore wide-brimmed hats. Most clothing was loose and free and thin, woven from fine wool. The loose cloak worn by everybody was known as a *chiton*. It could be tucked up short by workmen or wrapped around the body and worn to ground length by women. Both men and women wore leather sandals.

Education

In about 800BC, the Greeks improved a Phoenician alphabet by including vowels as well as consonants. Written language was then made much easier and it was possible for anyone to learn how to read and write. Written laws, argument, poetry and stories could replace or complement those that had been passed on orally, and a man's store of knowledge ceased being limited to the capacity of his memory. The advances made in Greek learning and literature owe much to this one invention.

Education was given only to boys from about 7 years of age and they were taught what we erroneously call the 'three Rs' – reading, writing and arithmetic. Like the Romans in a later period, the Greeks used a stylus (a sharp writing implement) pressed into a wax tablet to write down their work. Music, poetry and debating were also part of their education, and physical education was of major importance as a preparation for war. Rich families might have their girls privately educated but most learned only domestic tasks such as how to spin and weave.

The Olympic Games

Sport started as part of religious celebrations. The Olympic Games were invented by the Greeks over 2500 years ago (tradition has it, in 776BC). Sport and religion were mixed in a festival held every four years at Olympia to honour the god Zeus. In Roman times the growth of Christianity gradually killed off the old pagan festivals and the ancient Olympics were finally ended by the Roman Emperor Theodosius in AD371. The modern Olympic Games started in 1896 and the first were held in Athens. There were also games festivals held in Corinth – the Isthmian – and in Delphi – the Nemean and the Pythian. Collectively these festivals are known as the Panhellenic Games. Throughout the 5th century BC the Olympics were the biggest competition of all and lasted for five days. Even wars sometimes stopped to allow the games to take place

There were many similarities with today's Games. The athletes trained hard, had special diets and coaches and sometimes cheated. Cheats in the ancient Games were considered to have insulted the god. They were punished, if caught, by whipping-men and the city they represented was fined. You had to be Greek and a free man in order to compete in the games, which were an all-male affair – women could not even watch. Nudity was the norm (possibly as a means of making sure that no female could compete in disguise), physical prowess was much admired and the perfect body idolized in statues and paintings. Some historians believe that Spartan women competed regularly in their own athletic competitions. They certainly received physical training in order to build up their strength to produce fine babies.

Some of the events would still be recognized today, such as throwing the discus. Others, like the long jump, have changed a little – Greek long jumpers carried weights in their hands to help propel them a long distance. There were five key competitions in the Olympics: discus, javelin, wrestling, running and long jump; these made up the pentathlon. More and more events were added to the games – boxing and mud-wrestling were very popular, and after the battle of Marathon, the marathon was included as an event. Winners were awarded a palm branch and large jars of oil. Then, on the final day of the games, they were crowned with olive wreaths. Athletes winning three or more events were allowed to have a statue put up in their honour with an inscription that recorded their success.

In their own words

Because the people of Elis were the organizers of the Olympic Games, they had an agreement with the rest of the Greeks that their city was to remain sacred and free from attack; as a result they were complete strangers to war and everything it entails.
Polybios V, 2nd century BC

Greek theatre

Theatre also has its origins in a religious festival, the first drama festival being held in Athens in 534BC as part of the festival City Dionysia. Gradually plays moved away from religion and drama became a separate art in its own right. Some Greek plays have survived and are still performed, for example, *The Orestia*, *Tales from Ovid*, *Frogs* and *Phaedre*. At Epidauros in the east of the Peloponnese is the best-preserved Greek theatre. This massive auditorium could seat 14 000 and has become a modern tourist attraction that reminds us of the scale of interest the theatre must have generated.

Dramatic competitions were first held, rather like the Olympic Games, as part of religious festivals. Tragedies and comedies were performed on a flat area called the *orchestra*, at the base of an amphitheatre. No more than three actors spoke to each other at a time, so to avoid confusing the audience and ensuring that all actors could be heard. A large group of actors (the chorus), would speak to the audience directly and comment on the play's action. Women were probably not allowed to attend or to take part. The actors wore thick-soled shoes, tall wigs and padded clothes to make themselves bigger and more visible. Happy characters wore bright clothes, while criminals and unlucky characters wore grey, green or blue clothes and those in mourning wore black. Gods and goddesses carried wands and tridents and hunters always carried a purple shawl around their left arm. The actors wore masks made of clay to indicate the character and feelings of the role they were playing. All the masks had large gaping mouths that helped the actors to project their voices. Wigs and false beards were attached to the masks.

In their own words

His mother first, being high priestess, now began the kill, and rushed at him. Caressing her cheek he said, 'Mother it is I.'
The Bacchae, Euripedes, 5th century BC

Why you need to know these facts

It is necessary to know what Greek society was like in order to understand the achievements of the Ancient Greeks, and why their civilization still influences the ways of the world today.

Amazing facts

● The Greeks had no sugar but used sweet figs and honey instead.
● Greek words linger in the language of learning today – if a little changed in their meaning. Examples include Teacher (*grammatistes*); slave to escort pupils (*paidogogos*); training ground (*gymnasia*).
● A modern discus weighs about 2 kilograms. In ancient times it weighed 5 kilograms.
● The survival of Greek plays is amazing, although given the enormous number of plays that must have been written it is also a matter of some amazement that so few have survived. Thirty-five tragedies by Aeschylus, Sophocles and Euripides, and a few comedies, mainly by Aristophanes, are all that remain.

Teaching ideas

● With the class, stage a mini-Olympics (clothed, of course). You could include events like the standing jump. Have a trumpet to start and stop the races, dig footholds for the runners as starting blocks; add the speeches, poetry readings and dancing that was also part of the Games.
● Using clay as the base, get the children to model the grotesque features of a Greek theatre mask. Cover in Vaseline and then build up the mask using papier mâché.

● Tell the children to write a sports report of the Olympic Games describing the atmosphere as well as the events.

● Read a Greek myth about the actions of the gods to the class. Get the children to tell the story in another form – DTP, comic strip, an assembly and so on.

● Women in Ancient Greece had a rough deal by our standards. Tell the children to design a 'women's lib' pamphlet listing all the ways that women were poorly treated and arguing for change.

● Collect pictures of Greek ruins for a display. Have a debate about whether the ruins should be preserved or allowed to decay. (The Acropolis is falling down so this is a real problem.)

● On a large-scale map of the centre of your town or high street, mark in all the architectural references to Greek ideas. You could use a digital camera to make a photographic record that could be added to using a word processor to make a guide to the Greek legacy in your town.

● As an art project, make a replica Greek vase. You can use a balloon as the base, cover it in Vaseline and build up the shape using papier-mâché. Black figure vases had the figures painted on in black whilst the background was left alone. Red figure vases did the reverse. You could simply draw or paint vase scenes using the correct colours.

Religion and festivals

Religion was a major guiding force for the Ancient Greeks. They had many gods and a great respect for traditions and rites. Respect for traditions was such that Athenian priests were not allowed to bring any innovation into worship and such an act could be punished by death. For example, an animal had to be carefully examined before it was chosen for sacrifice: its skin had to be the right colour, the sacrificial knife had to have a blade of the right shape, the animal's throat had to be cut in a certain way and its meat roasted using the correct type of wood.

Subject facts

The main religion was the worship of ancestors and heroes. By our standards the Greeks were very superstitious – the Spartans would never start an expedition before the full moon, and the Athenian fleet would never sail unless the statue of Pallas was re-gilded. Life was a regular round of sacrifice and worship.

The gods were a kind of family with human traits – gods

might covet, lust, and be angry or kind. They lived their own mythological lives and were not always watching what humans were doing. They lived on Mount Olympus, the highest mountain in Greece. The Greeks' relationship with their gods can best be summed up as 'we'll look after you if you'll look after us.'

Festivals were held to please the gods and some were extravagant celebrations. There were festivals to remember the dead, private festivals, agricultural festivals and festivals to celebrate the birthdays of the gods. The big Athenian celebrations were Panathenia (the All-Athens Festival) and City Dionysia. The latter was a theatrical celebration of drama and poetry. Festivals usually included sacrifices to the gods. This was considered a way of making some kind of contact to ask for favours or help. Gods each had their favourite animals, so cows were slaughtered to satisfy Athena and pigs for Demeter.

The main gods on Olympus were:
Zeus – responsible for thunder, lightning and the weather. Father of many of the other gods and also of legendary heroes. The king of gods.
Poseidon – responsible for the sea and earthquakes; Zeus's brother.
Demeter – responsible for earth and agriculture; the oldest god.
Athena – goddess of Athens and goddess of wisdom.
Hermes – responsible for messages, travellers and good luck.
Apollo – responsible for music, hunting and curing disease.
Aphrodite – goddess of love, beauty and light. Mother of Cupid.
Artemis – goddess of birth, magic and the moon.
Ares – god of war.
Hephaistos – responsible for art and craftsmen; blacksmith god.
Hestia – the goddess of hearth and home.

Not on Olympus, but also important were:
Hades – king of the underworld.
Dionysus – god of wine, drugs and dancing (the first plays at festivals were held in his honour).
The oracle at Delphi – consulted by people from all over the Greek world. It was the oldest and most important oracle. It was said that Zeus sent two eagles to find the centre of the earth and that they met at Delphi. Alexander the Great is thought to have visited the oracle at Delphi and was told, 'My son, none can resist thee'.

Greek religious ideas need to be studied in order to understand the Greeks. But Greek religion was also a stimulus for developments that remain parts of our lives today. For example, the Olympic Games and the modern theatre both have their origins in Greek religious festivals.

● As each child to design a logo for a chosen god, making sure that it portrays the characteristics that the god would have exhibited.
● Compile a class dictionary of Greek gods.
● Ask the children to write a newspaper report describing festival celebrations in honour of a Greek god.
● As a class, design a Web page for the oracle at Delphi, advertising what it has to offer.

Teaching ideas

The city-state

The civilization of Ancient Greece was based upon the city-state, an idea that developed very fast, largely because of the dictates of geography. Small communities, often isolated by the mountainous nature of the landscape and limited usable space, established strong identities. Most Greek cities were no more than 5000 strong in population, although 5th century Athens had a voting population of up to 60 000. The democratic ideal was that every citizen had a vote, there were common laws, and a degree of self-sufficiency. Women did not count as citizens and neither did slaves – they had no rights and could not vote.

Subject facts

What were the city-states?
Athens was the largest and most densely populated city-state. It also tended to be the most powerful, mainly because it had good access to the sea through the port of Piraeus. Athens was a great colonizer and was interested in trade and sea power. It was also the civilized centre of the Greek world in the 5th century and was the centre of great art, literature and thought. Although in 480BC it was destroyed by the Persians, it was rebuilt on a grand scale under its leader Pericles. Athena, goddess of war and wisdom, was its patron and an owl its symbol.

Sparta was land-locked and a more introverted place. Great emphasis was placed upon military prowess, and Spartan boys had an upbringing of legendary harshness.

Sparta was ruled by a council of elders, and had an assembly of citizens which took decisions by public acclamation. But its government was not democratic in the Athenian style and was generally marked by rigid authoritarianism. Ultimately, Spartan government was controlled by two kings: they held military power and could overrule the assembly and the council. Fearing no one, their city was unwalled, for according to one Spartan leader, 'It is men, not walls, that make a city'.

Sparta competed for Greek dominance with Athens, although there were times when Sparta and Athens formed an alliance, most notably to defeat the Persian invaders in 480 and 479BC. During the early part of the 4th century, Sparta was the paramount state, having overshadowed Athens, but its leadership was inept, tyrannical and brutal. Its supremacy was ended with defeat by Thebes in 371BC. After this the Greek states slipped into their old ways of isolation and rivalry until the coming of Philip and Alexander of Macedonia.

Democracy

Athenian democracy in the 5th century had at its pinnacle the Assembly, which consisted of all male citizens over 18 years of age that were willing to attend the sessions held every ten days. Whatever the people decided in the Assembly was law. To encourage attendance the state police often did a sweep of the surrounding area and took people along. The system worked partly because the citizens took their responsibilities seriously, and partly because there were checks and controls built into the system. A steering committee of 500 citizens made recommendations as to how the Assembly should vote. Membership of the steering committee or Council was chosen by lot from lists of names nominated by each of the 10 electoral districts of Athens.

Warfare

Throughout the Classical period, warfare, or the threat of warfare was never far away. Either the Greeks were facing the external threat posed by the Persians, or they were involved in internal struggles for dominance of the Greek mainland. Persia had a powerful expanding empire and, under Darius I in the late 5th century BC, tried to conquer Greece. The Greek states were themselves becoming both more powerful and more independently minded, so conflict was inevitable. In 490BC, Darius's army was defeated by the Athenians at the battle of Marathon. But in

481BC his son Xerxes set out with a huge army and navy to avenge his father's defeat. The Spartans faced the Persians at Thermopylae in 480BC. Their army was decimated and Athens was then seized and destroyed. But the Athenians retained their fleet and, with their allies, confronted the Persians just west of Athens at Salamis in the same year. The Athenian naval victory was decisive and the Persians were finally forced to leave Greece for good.

Athens was left all-powerful amongst the Greek states, but sporadic struggles for power continued over the years. In 431 a huge conflict amongst powerful alliances of Greek cities (led by Athens and Sparta respectively) broke out. It lasted for 30 years and is known as the Peloponnesian War. The pendulum of fortune swung both ways, but Athens' surrender in 404BC was the end of the main conflict.

In their own words

In a night engagement how could anyone know anything for certain? Although there was a bright moon, they saw each other only as men do by moonlight. They could not tell for certain whether they were friends or enemies. After being thrown into disorder, they ended by coming into collision with each other in many parts of the field, friends with friends, and citizens with citizens, and not only terrified one another, but even came to blows. In the pursuit many lost their lives by throwing themselves over the cliffs, for the path down from Epipolae was narrow. Thucydides, 5th century BC

The city-state was at the heart of Ancient Greece. Much of the civilized development of Greece, particularly the evolution of its political ideas that are with us today, was due to the unique way that the city-state developed.

Why you need to know these facts

● Xerxes's expedition to Greece reputedly consisted of over 100 000 men and 1000 ships.
● Greek war galleys called triremes were propelled by oars as well as by sails and the largest galleys had three decks of oarsmen, as many as 150 in total. A reinforced prow was used to ram the enemy, but the sides of the galleys were very vulnerable to counter-ramming by the enemy. The Athenian fleet had as many as 300 triremes at one time.

Amazing facts

● The combined population of all the city-states was probably less than 500 000 – less than most modern cities.

Common
misconceptions

Everyone had a vote in ancient Athens and democracy was therefore in its purest form at that time.
In fact this kind of total democracy applied only to an elite. If you were excluded from this elite, by virtue of being a slave or a woman, for example, you had no democratic rights.

Teaching ideas

● Investigate the meanings of words of Greek origin 'then and now' (use the list given in the vocabulary section to start with). How have some meanings changed? Some modern words have a root meaning that is from Ancient Greek, for example *democracy* (rule of the people).
● Tell the class they are to plan a holiday in Greece to visit the ancient sites. Using brochures from travel agents, they should write guides to the sites.
● Explore some Greek discoveries and scientific ideas such as Archimedes' principle or the sieve of Eratothenes.
● Establish a 'shadow' democratic government for the running of your class based upon the Athenian model. Tell the children to draw lots for the Council. Will they exclude females? What rules could it make or what issues could it discuss? Try it for a week.

Famous Greeks

Subject facts

Alexander the Great
In the 4th century BC, a vacuum of leadership amongst the Greek states was filled from an unexpected quarter: Macedonia in the north. With the Greek states severely weakened after the Peloponnesian War, Philip II saw his chance to expand his empire. In 338BC following a decisive victory in the battle at Chaeronea, he seized control of the Greek states. He was assassinated two years later (the finger of suspicion is pointed at Alexander) and Alexander – his son – inherited the new kingdom when he was only 20 years of age.

Alexander eventually earned the title 'Great' due to his astonishing military exploits. He not only dominated Greece but went on to attack the Persian Empire, finally defeating Darius III in a bloody battle at Gaugamela in 331BC. He created a huge empire across Egypt, Afghanistan and Persia to the borders of India. In 327 he crossed the Himalayas, but his army was exhausted and his conquests came to an end. He died in 323BC – perhaps of malaria but more likely of poison – in Babylon. He was only 33 years old.

Alexander's greatness tends to rest on his military prowess, which is indisputable. However, some historians think that by the end of his life he was probably an insane alcoholic megalomaniac. But nevertheless his impact on the Greek world was immense. He took Greek culture and influence to places previously barely known. He also brought back to Greece an enormous amount of information about plants, people, mineral resources, geography and exotic cultures. Many surveyors and 'scientists' accompanied his military expeditions. This Greek intercourse with the East changed the face of the known world even though his empire collapsed shortly after he died.

In their own words

Be a leader to the Greeks and a despot to the barbarians, look after the former as friends and relatives, and deal with the latter as with beasts or plants.
Advice to the young Alexander from Aristotle

Other famous Greeks

Aspasia – women were usually uneducated, but Aspasia, the companion of the statesman Pericles, was famed for her intellect and judgement.

Demosthenes – a renowned Greek orator, lawyer and politician. Struggled to rouse the Athenians to the Macedonian danger. Died c413BC by taking poison after capture by the Macedonians.

Euclid – a Greek mathematician, taught in Alexandria around 300BC. His book *Elements* is a standard work of geometry.

Homer – responsible for the first great works of Greek literature – the *Iliad* and the *Odyssey* – written around the 8th century BC. Nothing is known about Homer himself.

Lycurgus – credited with having created the unique government of Sparta. May be a figure of legend only.

Oedipus – a character in the famous tragedy by Sophocles, King Oedipus unknowingly kills his father and marries his mother.

Pericles – a politician, statesman and general who led Athens during its period of imperial dominance. He introduced payment for people holding public office, rebuilt

Athens after its destruction by the Persians, and is responsible for the Parthenon.

Pheidias – an Athenian sculptor whose statues adorn the Acropolis in Athens.

Sappho – a female poet, lived around 600BC on the island of Lesbos near modern Turkey. Her poetry was mainly personal, dealing with her friendships and feuds with other women.

Xenophon – known for his historical writing, but wrote widely on topics from horsemanship to politics. He came from Athens but spent many years in the service of Sparta.

Why you need to know these facts

The achievements of the Ancient Greeks are partly remembered through the work and actions of significant individuals, many of whom influenced not only the ancient world, but also the world today.

Amazing facts

● Alexander the Great took his army on a march of 35 400 kilometres (22 000 miles), to Persia, the Caspian Sea, India and Bokhara.
● Alexander killed his best friend Clitus in a drunken rage.

Common misconceptions

Alexander is said to have founded 70 new cities.
This is an exaggeration, but one of his successors, Seleucus, created at least 59.

Teaching ideas

● Make a class presentation on the life of Alexander the Great, explaining why he was called 'Great'. Include a map of his journeys. How many towns were named after him? (There are eleven in Asia Minor and the Middle East alone.)
● With the class, mark on an outline map the travels of Alexander. Calculate the distance he travelled. Can you get close to the estimated 35 400km?
● Ask the children to research what the soldiers in the Greek and Persian armies looked like. Get the children to make recruiting posters for each army.

Books

Because the written record is extensive you will be able to quote selectively from a variety of Ancient Greek writers. For example, Thucydides' *The History of the Peloponnesian War*. Accessible retellings of Greek myths and legends are available that can be read to or by the children: *Greek Myths* by Lucilla Burn (British Museum Press) is a good authoritative source.

See also:
The Faber Book of Greek Legends; Greek Heroes and Monsters by Mason (Faber).
Entitlement to Classics Greek and Latin Programme, produced by the Open School, Park Road, Totnes, Devon TQ9 6EQ – contains some very useful teaching material.

Other useful reference books:
Sporting Success in Ancient Greece and Rome by Audrey Briers (Ashmolean Museum) – detail on the Olympics.
The World of Odysseus by Neil Grant (BBC) – a children's guide, brief but wide-ranging.
The Usborne Encyclopedia of Ancient Greece (Usborne) – finely illustrated overview, child-friendly.
The Greek and Persian Wars by Jack Cassin-Scott (Osprey Men-at-Arms Series) – excellent for those who want the gory detail, good maps and illustrations of armour.
Ancient Greece by Anne Pearson (Dorling Kindersley) – written in association with the British Museum, so a good mix of reliability and quality.
The Acropolis by Jane Shuter (Heinemann) – a different approach, lovely photographs, child-friendly.
Life in Ancient Greece by Sophia Sackville-West (Reader's Digest) – good teacher's guide.

Collecting

Postcards and holiday photographs are worth collecting as Greece is a popular holiday destination. Ask the children. Holiday brochures from travel agents are worth a browse.

Visits

The British Museum (020 7636 1555) – note the building's classical style – produces an activity book for children on the Ancient Greeks.
Ashmolean Museum Oxford (01865 278000).
Fitzwilliam Museum Cambridge, Greek galleries (01223 332900).

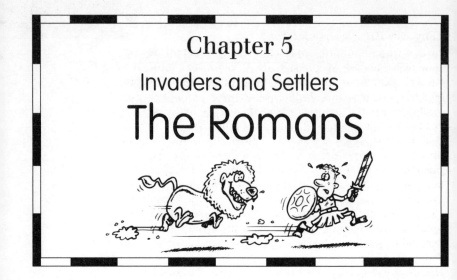

Chapter 5

Invaders and Settlers

The Romans

B efore studying the Romans in any depth, it is important to understand that they were the first of a number of foreign invaders who settled in the British Isles in the first millennium AD. This pattern of invasion and settlement largely dictated the unique characters of Wales, Scotland, Ireland and England.

Invasion and settlement

Subject facts

The movement and re-settlement of peoples is a natural process that can be seen continuously in all places across the globe. This intermingling of peoples and cultures has shaped, and continues to shape, Britain today.
Generally, invasions take place when:
● the invaders expect to gain something
● the invaders feel that they have a good chance of success.
Ask of the Romans, Saxons or Vikings, 'What did they stand to gain from invasion?', 'Why did they expect to be successful?' and you will begin to discover the underlying reasons for their attacks upon Britain.

Why was Britain invaded?

Britain was a tempting prospect for many invaders. At the time of the Roman conquest, Britain's main attraction lay in its agricultural and mineral wealth. Fertile soils produced rich harvests of wheat, and minerals such as iron, silver and gold were not only exported but also worked by Celtic craftsmen into useful and decorative artefacts.

Rome was the most powerful state in the Mediterranean and its well-organized army, led by ambitious generals, pushed forward the expansion of the Empire bringing success, wealth and power. Britain was seized in AD43, during a period of Roman expansion. When the Roman Empire eventually ceased expanding at the end of the 1st century, stone barriers (such as Hadrian's Wall) were erected to keep the Barbarians out.

But the Empire did not last forever. Another wave of invaders attacked Britain – Germanic tribes (Anglo-Saxons) who were themselves under pressure from the westward movement of people in central Asia. The western Roman Empire was attacked by Huns and, from about AD440 (some 30 years after the withdrawal of the Roman Legions from Britain) the coastal areas of eastern and southern England were settled by Angles and Saxons. They sought safe and fertile land to set up homes and start new lives. As the defences of Roman Britain weakened, they came in increasing numbers. Over a period of time they came, conquered and settled.

Then, in the 9th and 10th centuries, when western Europe was under attack from Magyars, Saracens and Vikings, Anglo-Saxon Britain became a tempting prize for Viking raiders. They shocked the English by sharing out their conquered land, settling on it, and starting to farm.

Each of these successive waves of peoples settled and integrated to some extent with the indigenous population. None wiped out the existing population completely, and all contributed to the cultural and linguistic heritage of the British.

Understanding our own world is made easier if we see the development of our nation as a continuous process of settlement. In many ways this began with the invasion of the Anglo-Saxons – unlike the Romans they did not pack their bags and leave. But the Roman invasion and settlement marked Britain's first major encounter with the civilized world, and thus is essential to children's understanding.

Why you need to know these facts

Introducing the Romans

Who were the Romans?

Rome was originally a tiny village 24 kilometres (15 miles) from the Mediterranean Sea in what is now Italy. It grew slowly, over 1000 years, into a huge cosmopolitan city with a population of about one million by the 2nd century AD. From these small beginnings, the Romans created one of the world's greatest empires and eventually, in AD212, granted Roman citizenship to every free person within the borders of the Empire. A Roman citizen might therefore come from Greece or North Africa, and might be black- or white-skinned.

Timeline

55BC	*Caesar lands in Britain*
54BC	*Caesar lands again*
43	*Claudius invades, Caractacus defeated and Colchester entered in triumph*
50	*Caractacus captured*
51	*Caractacus taken to Rome*
60	*Boudica, Queen of the Iceni, revolts*
78	*Agricola becomes governor of Britain*
84	*Mons Graupius – Romans defeat the Celts in Scotland*
122	*Hadrian visits Britain; the start of the wall*
180	*Romans content to retreat behind Hadrian's Wall*
360	*Picts and Scots cross the wall and invade*
410	*Legions leave to defend Rome*
c436	*Last Roman troops leave*

The ROMAN EMPIRE: AD117

Why do we need to know about the Romans?

The Romans irrevocably affected the landscape of Britain, the pattern of its roads and of its settlements. Moreover, Latin, the language of Rome, made a significant contribution to the development of the English language. Latin was for many years the language of all official documents and the language of educated people. Our language and laws remain peppered with phrases and structures that are Latin. The Romans also have to be studied, although not necessarily in depth, as part of the National Curriculum at Key Stage 2.

How do we know about the Romans?

The Roman legacy is huge and we can find evidence of their lives from sources such as:
● Ancient authors: for example Apicius (writer of a cookbook); Cato (wrote a book on agriculture); Josephus (a historian); and Pliny (prolific writer on all sorts of topics who wrote an encyclopedia of natural science).
● Legal documents and laws such as 'The Law Code of Theodosius'.
● Inscriptions (all types, including graffiti).
● Papyri (Rome annexed Egypt in 30BC but it was previously ruled by Macedonian kings, so Roman papyri are mostly written in Greek).
● Archaeological sites – huge amphitheatres, columns, arches and aqueducts still stand, but there are thousands of smaller sites, and many survive in Britain.

What happened to the Romans?

When Rome itself was threatened with attack, the legions stationed in Britain were gradually withdrawn. In AD410 the Emperor Honorius wrote to the provinces of Britain instructing towns to 'look to their own defence', and Roman rule in Britain was effectively over. However, a large Romano-British population remained, and the old Roman town life continued for many years. But as the Saxon raiders started to settle in Britain, a new order replaced the old, and Saxon settlements grew up alongside decaying Roman ones.

● The frontiers of the Roman Empire (as shown on the map opposite) were defended by over 300 000 men.

Amazing facts

Vocabulary

Ballista – small catapult firing iron missiles.
Hill Fort – a hilltop fortified by ramparts and ditches. Used by the Celts against the Romans.
Onager – a giant catapult used by the legions to fire a missile over 400 metres – usually ten of these to a legion.
Basilica – a Roman public hall used for administration with a double row of columns, aisles down the sides and an apse at one end, this set the pattern for the Christian churches.
Forum – an open rectangular space that was the centre of business in a Roman town. Also a marketplace.
Hypocaust – the Roman method of providing under-floor heating. Warm air circulated in channels beneath the floor and between walls.

The Roman occupation of Britain

Subject facts

Conquering the Celts

Britain was inhabited by tribes of Celts at the time of the Roman invasions. It was situated on the outer fringe of the Empire and was one of the last provinces to be acquired by the Romans.

Julius Caesar had made two invasions of Britain, in 55 and 54BC, but did not stay to conquer. By the time of Emperor Claudius and the final invasion in AD43, trading links with the Empire had already been established.

Cunobelinus (Shakespeare's Cymbeline) had been the most powerful Celtic leader and was friendly to the Romans, but he died in AD40 and his son, Caractacus was anti-Roman. Rome wanted a politically stable Britain, and conquest was one way of ensuring that it got it.

The invasion began when 40 000 men crossed from Boulogne commanded by Aulus Plautius. The four legions were the IInd Augusta, XIVth Gemina, XXth Valeria Victrix and IXth Hispana. The army soon overcame local resistance and captured Camulodunum (Colchester).

Claudius was lauded in Rome as a great champion and an arch was erected claiming he had defeated eleven kings. In Britain the conquest continued, one army going towards Lincoln, another towards Leicester and a third towards the south-west. The great Celtic hill fort of Maiden Castle near Dorchester was captured, roads and fortresses were built, local tribes disarmed, and any revolt ruthlessly put down.

Resistance to the Roman occupation

Moving westwards and northwards proved difficult for the
Roman legions and it took a series of hard campaigns
lasting over a decade. The XXth legion, from its forward
base in Gloucester, moved into north Wales, but success in
battle was not enough to subdue local resistance as the
establishment of forts throughout the west and south shows.
The Romans' biggest success came through treachery,
when the Queen Cartimandua of the Brigantes handed over
Caractacus, the leader of British resistance, to the Romans.

Caractacus

Caractacus (Caradoc) fought for seven years against the
Romans and was a major thorn in their side. Unfortunately,
opposition against the Romans was never united and the
tribes squabbled amongst themselves. Some tried to curry
favour with the invaders, and Cartimandua's treachery was
probably done for this reason. Caractacus' last battle, near
Ludlow, was a disastrous defeat. Cartimandua betrayed
him, and the following year (51) he was taken to Rome to be
put on show by the Emperor Claudius. It is thought that he
died there about three years later.

Boudica

In AD60, just when Anglesey had been captured and the
Romans had at last achieved success in the west, they paid
the penalty for arrogance and poor government in the east.
Queen Boudica, leader of the Iceni, led a revolt that came
within a whisker of success.

The Iceni and the Trinovantians had suffered 20 years of
heavy taxation and bullying under the Romans. The veteran
soldiers who settled at Camulodunum were particularly
aggressive, taking and settling on native land. In AD60
Boudica suffered more humiliation and her daughters were
raped. Enough was enough. The tribes rose up under her
leadership and attacked Colchester, London and St Albans,
slaughtering the Romans they encountered and burning the
cities to the ground. They were virtually unopposed until
they turned northwards to meet a small force of 10 000 men
under the commander Suetonius Paulinus. The huge tribal
army was no match for the discipline and military skill of
the Roman army. Boudica's force was routed, some 80 000
were killed and Boudica herself is thought to have taken
poison rather than be captured.

The Romans took bloody revenge, but they had learned
an important lesson and a wiser, more benign regime was
installed to govern the area.

Agricola took over the governorship of Britain in AD78 and was the most successful and energetic of the Roman rulers. He completed the conquest of Britain, subduing north Wales and pushing forward northwards to the River Forth by AD80. Many forts were established and the final campaign took the Romans to victory against the British in AD84 at Mons Graupius in north-east Scotland. But the north was never to be fully subdued or settled, and by AD100 garrisons had been withdrawn to a defensive position along a line where Hadrian was eventually to build his wall.

In their own words

Each soldier trains every day with all his energy as if in war. It would not be wrong to call their practice sessions bloodless battles and their battles bloody practice sessions.
'A history of the Jewish War', Josephus (AD37–c100)

Building Hadrian's Wall

At one time, the idea of building a wall around the Empire would not have been entertained, because the Romans felt invincible and believed that their Empire knew no boundaries. But the world changed. The Emperor Hadrian visited Britain in 122 and the construction of the wall began with a view to keeping out the barbarian tribes from the north. The wall was built of stone, although some of it was originally a turf rampart which was later replaced. Except where the landscape provided its own natural defence, a deep ditch was dug on the north side.

It was originally intended to build milecastles along the length of the wall. The scheme was not completed, but 16 auxiliary forts were added. The defensive force on the wall was probably 9 000 men; additional defences were built on the vulnerable coastal fringes at either end of the wall. The legionnaries themselves undertook all the building work.

Hadrian's Wall:
● defined a military zone where all movement could be controlled (there were ditches behind and in front of the wall)
● regulated trade through a few well-guarded gateways, where arms were confiscated and custom duties collected
● provided collecting places at the forts for intelligence about unrest beyond the frontier
● provided a military base from which attacks could be launched northwards.

For about ten years up to 155, Hadrian's wall took second place to the Antonine Wall which was about 60 kilometres (37 miles) long and stretched roughly between Glasgow and Edinburgh 128 kilometres (80 miles) to the north.

We need to know about the conquest to understand how the Romans came to dominate land and people with such relatively small forces.

● The Emperor Claudius himself led the Roman army in triumph into Camulodunum accompanied by elephants.
● Hadrian's Wall is one of the engineering wonders of the ancient world, if only because of its sheer size. It ran for 80 Roman miles (73 English miles or 117 kilometres) from Bowness in the west to Wallsend in the east. The wall became the northern boundary of the Roman Empire for 250 years.

The British warrior queen was called Boudicea.
Although this is still an accepted rendering of her name, it actually stems from a Victorian mis-reading of the evidence: Boudicca, Boudica or even Bonduca are preferred. Following the modern trend not to double consonants where there is a choice (for example, focused not focussed), Boudica is gaining the widest currency.

● Encourage the children to use the Internet to research the Romans. Get them to use this information to create a travel agent's guide to the main Roman tourist attractions such as Pompeii, Arles, Rome, Cirencester or St Albans.
● Try constructing working models of Roman siege engines like the onager and ballista.
● Produce a class timeline showing the main events of the Roman occupation of Britain.
● As a class, make a model of a Roman fort using historical evidence to help accuracy.
● For an assembly, perhaps, produce news and on-the-spot reports of the Roman campaign to conquer Britain. Include a report of the invasion. You could make this an audio experience with background music and sound effects.

Roman society

Towns

The development of towns took time and the first were
ramshackle establishments. But the Romans used the town
as a way of Romanizing the native population. They
encouraged tribal leaders to adopt Roman ways and educate
their children according to the Roman fashion. Wealthy
Romano-Britons were encouraged and helped to establish
settlements based near to Roman roads. Some towns were
specially planned to accommodate *colonia*, or settlements
of retired soldiers. (Colchester was developed as a *colonia*
although the site was an old tribal capital.) These places
took time to build properly (20 to 25 years) and might have
a town hall, a forum or market-place, temple, theatre,
senate house, comfortable town houses, amphitheatre and
sewered streets laid out in a grid plan. Most did not grow
beyond 160 hectares (100 acres) in size but they were
visible statements of Roman wealth, power and culture, and
the natives were attracted by the conveniences of their way
of life. London, on a site picked by Roman engineers for its
suitability as a trading port, grew to be a centre of
administration as well. By AD100 it was well-garrisoned as a
provincial capital and became something of a boom town.

Roads

Roads connected the towns of Roman Britain and were
essential for trade, the swift movement of troops and the
transport of the Imperial Post. Astonishingly well-
engineered, their remains are still visible today, and the
routes they established are still used. The Imperial Post ran
along the principal routes, some 16 routes radiating from
London, and had changing stations and rest houses at 19
kilometre (12 mile) stages. The local area was responsible
for keeping the roads in good order.

Villas

Villas were profit-making farms, not luxury holiday homes.
They could be small-scale and squalid, or extensive and
opulent. The richest examples in Britain were the centres of
small estates and these possessed courtyards and verandas
with imported marble sculptures and many rooms with
painted walls. Like villages or large houses of a later age,
villas changed and developed over time, and some became
small centres of manufacture specializing in producing
cloth or iron tools. Each villa would have had its own slave
workers, although evidence of the way they were housed

shows that the term 'slave' does not necessarily equate to the oppressed individuals of more recent times. Slavery was a normal part of ancient society; the term was used loosely and could cover people who rose to positions of considerable authority as well as those treated like chattels to be bought and sold.

Most Roman villas were built by wealthy, important natives who adopted the Roman way of life and by Roman immigrants and retired soldiers. They incorporated accommodation for slaves and workers, barns for storage and animals, wells for water and, in the later examples, their own bath houses and central heating.

Baths

In major Roman towns, the streets were laid out in rectangular blocks with a proper drainage system and good water supplies with public baths and lavatories. Public baths were part of Roman culture and they first appeared in the Roman towns of the south and west of England. Bath still has splendid remains of a system that was part functional, part cultural and part recreational. Individual villas had their own water systems, lavatories and baths, but in Bath we can see the provision at its grandest.

Baths were constructed with warm and hot rooms and cold plunges to stimulate the body. Many of the baths were richly decorated with mosaic-tiled floors. People found them pleasant places where they could pass an hour or two gossiping, swimming, having massages or playing games. The Romans made sure that they were clean by rubbing oil into their skin and then scraping the dirt and oil mixture off their skin using a blunt scraper called a strigil. While in the baths they might use the lavatories, which were sociable places with perhaps 16 people sitting side by side. Additional facilities, such as a hairdressers, shops and so on, that we find in modern retail and sport complexes were also provided in the larger baths.

The hottest room was the caldarium, which would bring you out in a heavy sweat, after which you would plunge into the frigidarium, or ice-cold pool. There were drains to take away dirty water from the baths and toilets. Most houses did not have drains, and a pot or bucket served as a toilet.

Religion

Subject facts

The Roman attitude to religion was similar to that of the Greeks: a practical matter; it did not involve much in the way of philosophy or emotion. It was a matter of ritual practices which would yield some benefit – a sort of trade with the gods. The Romans were generally very tolerant about religion, provided it posed no political threat. Native gods and local cults were allowed to co-exist with Roman deities, although the Romans made an exception of the Druids whom they bloodily persecuted because they perceived them to be a threat to Roman rule. Emperors were, after Augustus (27BC), given the status of god – generally after their deaths – and a temple was built in Colchester to the Emperor Claudius. The principal gods of the city of Rome itself were Jupiter, Juno and Minerva, and it was the custom to set up altars to Jupiter in the forts established in Britain. There is plentiful evidence in Britain of sacrifices to two popular gods, Mars (a warrior figure) and Mercury (god of trade and travel). After AD312 the Roman Empire was encouraged to become Christian and, as Christianity did not tolerate other gods, it put the other divinities under threat, although the worship of gods such as Mercury persisted for a long time.

In their own words

> *To Jupiter, best and greatest, the first cohort of Spaniards,
> which is commanded by Gaius Caballius Priscus, tribune.*
> An altar inscription at Maryport, Cumbria

Why you need to know these facts

Life in Roman Britain was unlike anything that had gone before. The first named Briton appears only through the annals of the Roman occupation. To understand what this country was like when it first appears on the pages of recorded history, we must understand the mundane and the ordinary; in short, how people lived their daily lives.

Amazing facts

● London (Londinium) covered an area of 130 hectares (325 acres) enclosed by walls, and was the biggest Roman city north of Italy.

● Every project on the Romans should include a close look at mosaics. There are various ways of making them, depending on available resources and the age of the children. You can make your own clay tesserae, fire and glaze them, then set them in plaster of Paris or thistle plaster. The mosaic effect can also be created using coloured squares of paper. Try to be authentic in your choice of colours (usually limited to blue, black, white, yellow and red). The children should study pictures of Roman mosaics carefully before they begin. Concentrate on a small section or examples of the standard geometric patterns that were used.

● Ask the children to try doing some arithmetic using Roman numerals. What happened to zero? Can they find ways of adding and subtracting?

● Teach some Latin. Some of the Cambridge Latin Course could be used with older pupils. Give the children some Latin roots to English words (for example, *decem* = ten) and let them trawl the dictionary or the spellchecker in their computer for words derived from them.

● Make a wax writing tablet. Construct a small wooden frame and use melted beeswax (use a microwave) for an authentic reproduction.

Resources

With so much emphasis being placed upon literacy, it is worth remembering that historical fiction is a useful source of inspiration, a way of appealing to children's imaginations and can provide a good backdrop to a topic. Authors such as Henry Treece, Geoffrey Trease and Rosemary Sutcliff (the famous *Eagle of the Ninth* (Puffin), for example) have written good quality fiction for children. *Eagle's Honour* by Rosemary Sutcliff (Red Fox) contains two stories suitable for most juniors. Also look at *Across the Roman Wall* by Theresa Breslin and *The Stone Street* by Marilyn Tolhurst (A&C Black). Ancient sources can be used selectively with children, for example *On Britain and Germany* Tacitus (Penguin) and *The Conquest of Gaul* Caesar (Penguin).

Primary history textbooks should not be overlooked as a resource because since the advent of the National Curriculum many excellent new ones have been produced.

Here are just a few of the many reference and resource books available that could be useful in the classroom:

Metropolis, Roman Town by HM Martell and M Bergin (Franklin Watts)
Sightseers, Ancient Rome by J Stroud (Kingfisher)
Roman Britain by TW Potter (British Museum)
Roman Legion by D Zienkiewicz (National Museum of Wales and the Ermin Street Guard)
Roman Crafts and Industries Shire Archaeology by P Johnson (Shire)
Food and Cooking in Roman Britain by M Woodman (Corinium Museum, Cirencester).

Trips

There are plenty of Roman sites to be found, even if Hadrian's Wall, Cirencester or York are too far away, there is a long list! Contact English Heritage for more information (020 7973 3000; www.english-heritage.org.uk). Don't overlook forts and reconstructions such as South Shields (west gate rebuilt); the Lunt, Baginton near Coventry (timber rampart and granary rebuilt). Almost every local museum will contain Roman finds so check what's on offer.

Maps

Ordnance Survey produces maps of Roman Britain, Hadrian's Wall and the Antonine Wall. In conjunction with various museums and trusts and the Royal Commission on Historical Monuments (RCHM), they also produce a number of special local maps including Londinium and Roman and Medieval Bath.

ICT

Computer programs and CD-ROMs on the Romans can be found in all good software catalogues (see AVP Educational Software, School Hill Centre, Chepstow, Gwent; 01291 625 439). Try *Arcventure I: The Romans* (Sherston); *Nag Burn* (Appian Way); *Zig Zag: The Romans* (Longman Logotron).

Re-enactments

A unique group of enthusiasts re-enact Roman military skills. They are 'The Ermine Street Guard', Oakland Farm, Dog Lane, Crickley Hill, Witcombe, Gloucester. They have produced some photographic material.

Role-play experiences are becoming increasingly popular and are being offered by a growing number of local groups. For example: *'Vitae Lampadae'*, Historical Education Services, 25 Rowan Close, Scarborough YO12 6NH. (01723 367 746) and Andrew Spooner (Living History) 01354 696 779 www.skylark-uk.com

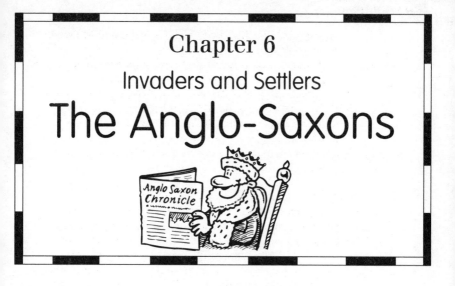

Chapter 6
Invaders and Settlers
The Anglo-Saxons

The Anglo-Saxons were one of a number of peoples who invaded and settled in the British Isles in the first millennium AD. It is necessary to understand this pattern of invasion and settlement not least because it largely dictated the unique and different characters of Wales, Scotland, Ireland and England.

Before studying the Anglo-Saxons in any depth, it is also important to understand why this invasion was only one of a number that occurred up to the Norman Conquest. The section 'Invasion and settlement' in Chapter 5 (page 66) details some of the underlying reasons behind these invasions and applies equally to the invasion by the Anglo-Saxons.

Introducing the Anglo-Saxons

Who were the Anglo-Saxons?

Subject facts

The Angles and Saxons were people of Germanic origin who came to Britain from areas in modern Germany and Denmark. There were many Germanic invaders – Saxons, Jutes, Franks, Frisians and Angles (the Mercians, Deirans and Bernicians were all called Saxons by the Celts). They were tribal people, closely bound to a group leader to whom they were fiercely loyal. The names of their leaders live on in English place names: Tota's people lived at Tooting, Wocca's at Wokingham, and Haefer's people at Havering.

	Timeline
CAD410	*Romans leave Britain to defend lands of their Empire closer to Rome.*
420	*Anglo-Saxons build the first houses at Stow, Suffolk.*
449	*Legends say that Anglo-Saxon leaders Hengist and Horsa arrive in Kent.*
563	*St Columba establishes a monastery on the Isle of Iona.*
577	*Battle of Dyrham near Bath. West Saxons conquer the Cotswolds.*
597	*St Augustine lands in Kent from Rome to convert the English to Christianity.*
625	*Sutton Hoo burial.*
663	*Conference at Whitby (Synod of Whitby); decision made to follow the Church of Rome.*
731	*Bede writes his* Ecclesiastical History of the English Nation.
735	*Death of Bede.*
	Vikings land in Dorset.
793	*Vikings sack the monastery on Lindisfarne.*
	Great Danish Army attacks England.
	Alfred becomes King of Wessex.
	Danish kingdom of York established.
	Alfred accepts the surrender of the Danes.
	Alfred captures London.
899	*Death of Alfred.*

Why do we need to know about the Anglo-Saxons?

The world of the 21st century is dominated by western culture and is increasingly tied together by the English language, which owes a considerable debt to the Anglo-Saxons. England has a pattern of settlement substantially dictated by the Saxon invaders. The Anglo-Saxons are a required element in the National Curriculum.

How do we know about the Anglo-Saxons?

The Anglo-Saxon period is often regarded as a confused and shadowy period of British history, a time of many kingdoms and little-known kings. Lying between the civilized culture of the Romans and medieval Christendom, it has often been called the 'Dark Ages'.

The main reason for this is the dearth of written evidence. What evidence there is comes from documents such as the *Anglo-Saxon Chronicle*, begun in the 800s by the monks of Winchester, which records the successes of the Saxons, but not their defeats. So our main sources are biased against the Celts and Romano-British.

Our main historical sources for this period are:

● Archaeological finds, especially those from Saxon cemeteries and the Sutton Hoo burial site in Suffolk.

● The *Anglo-Saxon Chronicle* (already mentioned above), written in English (Latin speakers had all but disappeared by the 9th century). It used the masterly innovation of dating events from the birth of Christ – AD (*Anno Domini*).

● Other written evidence, such as illuminated manuscripts like the *Lindisfarne Gospels*, poems such as *Beowulf* and the *Battle of Maldon*, and Bede's *Ecclesiastical History of England*.

● Architecture – there are significant remains of ecclesiastic buildings but no domestic buildings. Archaeology has enabled some reconstruction to take place such as that at West Stow near Bury St Edmunds.

● Place names (see page 84).

What happened to the Anglo-Saxons?

The Anglo-Saxons have never left and Britain is still sometimes referred to as an Anglo-Saxon country. The Anglo-Saxons' impact upon Britain was substantial, not just in language, culture and political geography, but in people. Recent DNA analysis of skeletal remains and comparisons with the DNA of existing inhabitants of Britain have found remarkable links: Celtic and Saxon roots can still be traced. For many people in Britain the answer to the question 'What happened to the Anglo-Saxons?' may therefore be at least partly answered by looking in the mirror. Anglo-Saxon genes may be present in you, as they form part of the racial foundation of many modern Britons.

Eventually the Saxon tribes settled down to live in peace with each other and with the remaining Celtic groups, and became more preoccupied with facing the common threat from the raiding northmen from Scandinavia. But they fought with, and eventually learned to live with, the Vikings, absorbing them into the English nation. The line of Saxon rulers, however, ends with Harold at the Battle of Hastings, and the coming of the Normans in 1066.

That the Anglo-Saxons were Angles (from Angulus between the lands of the Jutes and the Saxons) and Saxons (from what is now called Old Saxony).
Although this is broadly correct, Bede used the term generically to cover all the German invaders. The majority were Angles, Saxons and Jutes; there were also Frisans and possibly some Danes.

Common misconceptions

Vocabulary

Wessex – literally, the land of the West Saxons, ruled over at one time by Alfred and the centre of resistance to the Viking invaders. Centred on the southern counties of Wiltshire, Hampshire and Dorset.

Jutes, Saxons and **Picts** – using modern geographical terms, invaders from Jutland, Germany and Scotland.

Scabbard – a sheath for a sword.

Buckle – a metal fastening using a pin; remains have been found in grave burials when the material it fastened has rotted. A solid gold buckle was found at Sutton Hoo.

Wergeld – the price paid for killing a person, a blood price. The more important the person, the higher the price.

The invasion of the Anglo-Saxons

Subject facts

Mercenaries and early raiders

The first Saxons who came to Britain were mercenaries who had been invited by the Roman authorities to protect Britain from invasion by other Saxons. After the Romans left, the hiring of Germanic mercenaries continued, but some of these groups got out of control and started to carve out territory for themselves in the east. Tradition has it that a band of Jutes, led by the brothers Hengist and Horsa, were invited by a British leader called Vortigern in AD449 to help defend his kingdom against the Picts (from Scotland). They were given the Isle of Thanet in Kent as a reward, but they revolted and took the whole of Kent for themselves. The date is not certain – and the chroniclers who wrote about these events relied heavily on the writings of Bede, who finished his history in 731 – but there had been raids before this that the Romans had had to contend with and the Saxon raiders seem to have penetrated far inland by 429. But the beginning of settlement, at first it appears by peaceful agreement, was something different.

More and more Saxons from the pagan tribes of Western Europe started to come to Britain seeking land, and they began the process of establishing Saxon kingdoms. It is not certain which kingdom came first, but it was probably north of the River Tees, where Saxons had been employed to repel the Picts (from Scotland) and the Scots (from Ireland), that the kingdom of Deira developed.

For more than 100 years the British fought fiercely

against the invaders but they were forced to retreat westwards although, for a time, the Saxon advance was hindered by natural barriers such as the great forest of Selwood, which was 48 kilometres (30 miles) wide. The turning point in this part of English (for that is what the Saxons became) history was the battle at Dyrham, above Bath, in 577, when three British kings were killed and the cause of the Britons fatally damaged.

By the beginning of the 7th century, the Anglo-Saxons controlled most of what we now call England, plus parts of southern Scotland. One group of invaders, by no means the most important or dominant group, eventually gave their name to the country. The Angles gave us *Angle-land*, which later became England.

Saxon kingdoms

At first there were many Saxon kingdoms, but during the 7th century twelve small kingdoms were gradually reduced in number to the three powerful kingdoms of Mercia, Wessex and Northumbria. Offa, king of Mercia, had a dyke dug as a boundary between the English and the Welsh. It ran from the Irish Sea to the Bristol Channel and was 7.6 metres (25 feet) deep and 18 metres (60 feet) wide. The dominance of the Anglo-Saxons became absolute and today little remains of Celtic (British) place names or words in the English language.

Place names

The comprehensive nature of Anglo-Saxon invasion and settlement is clearly set out in the pattern of place names across the UK. Some natural features of the countryside have names of Celtic origin (the Mendips, Ouse, Usk and Exe), but most English place names are Saxon. There are certain endings that indicate Saxon origins. The prefix that accompanies these endings is usually personal, relating to the people whose migration ended there, or geographical, relating to some striking feature of the place. For example:

-ing – this comes from *ingas* and refers to groups of people
Hastings	Haest's people
Reading	Reada's people

-ham – denotes a settlement or homestead
Heysham	estate in a wood
Horsham	estate where horses are kept

-ingham – settlement/estate belonging to a group of people
Nottingham	estate of Snot's people
Gillingham	estate of Gylla's people

-ton or **-tun** – an enclosure or village
Hutton	farm on a hill
Everton	boar farm

-ington – a village belonging to a group of people
Donington	farm of the hill dwellers
Bickington	farm of Beocca's people

Why you need to know these facts

The so-called Dark Ages hold the key to understanding the landscape of Britain today. The pattern of settlement, as indicated by place names, provides a major clue to our Anglo-Saxon roots.

Amazing facts

The Saxons called the Britons *Welsh*, which was their word for foreigners. They did not kill all of the Welsh, or push them all into Wales and Cornwall; some co-existed with the Saxons. *Walton* (as in Walton-on-Thames or Walton-on-the-Wolds) means 'Welsh settlement'.

● On an outline map of England, get the children to mark with coloured dots place names ending in *-ing, -ton, -ington, -ham,* and *-ingham*. Investigate your local Saxon kingdom.

● On an outline map of Europe, show where the Anglo-Saxon raiders came from. Mark the Saxon shore of Britain and the sites of important Saxon battles.

● Ine, King of Wessex in 690, produced laws which give us some idea of the value placed on a Welshman, and also show that the Saxons and the Welsh co-existed. Wergeld was the compensation to be paid for the taking of a life: for an Englishman it was between 200 and 1200 shillings for killing a Welshman:

A Welsh slave	*50 shillings*
A landless Welshman	*60 shillings*
A Welsh rent-payer	*120 shillings*

In a class discussion, make a list of all the deductions you can make from this law of Ine about how the Saxons and Welsh treated each other.

Anglo-Saxon society

Life in an Anglo-Saxon village

Subject facts

The Saxons ignored the urban dwellings of the Romano-British and lived, for the most part, in small tribal settlements, closely bound to their leader. They built dwellings almost entirely of wood (their first stone buildings were religious) cut from the forests and woods that surrounded them. They used axes, saws and wedges to prepare the timber for use, and essentially built a house of planks, including planks for a floor with a space below for ventilation to keep the wood dry. Preferably the house faced south to catch the sun; it was roofed using sedge or reeds, and a fire inside would have been contained in a firebox lined with clay. The smoke would have wafted out through gaps between the roof and the eaves (a hole in the roof would have let the rain in and caused a down draught!) Villages were never far from a source of water, for obvious reasons, and everything else they needed came from the countryside around them. Medicines were made from herbs and the land was farmed for food. Surpluses were traded for their other needs such as iron and tools. In many ways the self-sufficiency of the Anglo-Saxon village was little different from the way of life of people in England until the Industrial Revolution. For example, pigs were very important animals because they were efficient providers of food, and this was true right up to Victorian times and, in a few cases, beyond.

Animal bones were used to make small items such as pins and combs (the Saxons were alive with lice and would have needed nit combs), and animal excrement was used for manure. Preservation of food over the winter months was a tricky business, for villagers had to fight with pests as well as with mould and decay. Food was mostly eaten in season, but some was pickled using liquids such as honey. Bread was pretty rough stuff, and grain ground by hand with a quern was sometimes mixed with acorns or seeds to make the flour go further. Almost everything was made at home. Wool was spun by hand and cloth woven on a wooden-framed loom in the house.

Life was driven by the seasons and the weather, so most of the time people were occupied with the struggle to stay alive. Life expectancy was not very high. But people still found time to make music, to sing and to tell stories in the main hall that served as the centre of every village.

Life and death
Dead Saxons were cremated and their ashes buried in a pot with some personal belongings such as a brooches. Sometimes the pots were decorated with runes. As the Saxons became Christian these practices changed and they were buried in consecrated ground without grave goods.

Writing
The Germanic invaders, like the Vikings later, used simple line designs called runes for writing. They also used Roman letters, and the Christian Saxons, such as Bede, used Latin for their manuscripts. The Christian and cultured world of 8th century Britain (the Dark Ages) produced the first writing in Old English.

Beowulf
The longest and most complete poem in Old English is *Beowulf.* It is a great heroic poem and an important historical document. It tells the story of a fiendish half-monster, Grendel, who lived in the fens of Denmark and has killed many warriors. Beowulf sails to Denmark with 14 men to assist him in the fight against the monster. The bloody tale unfolds, and ends with the triumph of the hero.

Beowulf becomes king for 50 years, but is killed by a dragon; his body is burned in the Germanic tradition and his men wreak vengeance on the dragon. *Beowulf* was part of the Saxons' oral tradition. It was probably written down when the Anglo-Saxons converted to Christianity (there are several references to the new religion).

Learning about the pattern of Anglo-Saxon life is important, not only because it teaches us about the Anglo-Saxons, but also because we learn about a pattern of daily life that continued for ordinary people, with very little change, for a thousand years or more. The beginnings of English, now a key world language, also lie here.

Teaching ideas

● Act out the story of *Beowulf* with sound effects and using extracts from the poem. Alternatively, as a class, create a storyboard, retelling the tale as if for the making of a film.
● Using an appropriate medium, make your own Beowulf.
● The Saxons enjoyed playing with words. Investigate Anglo-Saxon riddles. Encourage the children to make up some of their own.
● Make a class model of an Anglo-Saxon village using information from West Stow.

Religion

Conversion to Christianity

Subject facts

The Saxons were pagans, and came with their own gods to an island that had been part of the Christian Roman Empire. They sacked Christian churches, but did not impose their gods on the British. We can tell that the British held on to their pagan beliefs for some time from the pagan burials that reveal grave goods not found in Christian graves.

Celtic Christianity survived, but only on the western fringes of Britain, in Ireland and in monasteries in places like Iona, founded by St Columba. Because, in the end, Christianity triumphed, we have less evidence about the pagan beliefs of the Saxons, although they have a sometimes unnoticed influence upon our culture today. Easter, for example, is named after the goddess Eostre about whom nothing else is known. Pagan winter festivals and fertility beliefs were blended in to Christian practices – Easter eggs, yule logs and so on.

In 597, the same year that St Columba died, St Augustine – a Roman missionary sent by Pope Gregory the Great – landed at Thanet, Kent. His mission was to convert the heathens to Christianity. His tactic was a top-down one: to begin by converting the rulers first, on the principle that the rest of the people would follow. Landing in Kent he sent emissaries to inform King Ethelbert of his arrival and sought an audience.

Politically, Ethelbert may have seen it as a good move to encourage Augustine, but the meeting must also have been an intellectual and theological mismatch: a religion of little theology had to face one whose subtleties had been worked on by the great thinkers of Rome. Ethelbert listened thoughtfully, but he did not overthrow the heathen temples. Instead, he allowed Augustine to repair the Romano-British churches and to preach his message to the people. Augustine was totally dependent upon Ethelbert's support such that the Kent town of Canterbury remains, to this day, the world centre of the Anglican communion.

Augustine was able to send missionaries around the country, and also arranged to meet the leaders of what was left of the British Church. He demanded that they follow the Roman pattern of worship, in particular, that they adopt the same date for Easter. The British Church is said to have taken exception to his authoritarian tone and rejected his overtures. Augustine died around 604, having become the first Archbishop of Canterbury, but not having managed to spread Christianity far beyond the borders of Kent. Moreover, a rift had been established between the Roman and Celtic traditions.

The spread of Roman Christianity throughout Britain took a century. The conversion of the North and Midlands was largely due to Celtic missionaries from Iona, so the two traditions of Christianity developed in competition. As various kings gave a Christian lead – notably Oswy, King of Northumbria – Christianity came to dominate the land, but the Celtic-Roman clash remained unresolved. King Oswy convened a meeting at Whitby in 664 to settle the matter (known as the Synod of Whitby). The meeting was acrimonious. In the end, the final sticking point was the date of Easter. The King gave his support to the Roman date and the Celtic representatives withdrew disgruntled. The most powerful King in Britain at the time decided the issue. Britain henceforth came within the orbit of Rome, and King Oswy and his wife were able to celebrate Easter on the same date – which, coming from different traditions, they had not been able to do until the decision of the Synod.

In their own words

Our Easter customs are observed in all the world except by the Scots and their obstinate supporters the Picts and British.
Wilfrid, Abbot of Ripon speaking at the Synod of Whitby 664

Monks and nuns

The monastic life was a layman's quest for spiritual purity, and consisted largely of prayer and contemplation. It began with St Benedict, who was born in central Italy around AD500. He eschewed luxuries, like a soft bed and rich food, and withdrew from public life. He eventually organized a community of monks, gave up worldly pleasures, and wrote the *Benedictine Rule* for monks to live by.

The Celtic version of monasticism tended towards the hermit life, which was particularly popular in Ireland. But, encouraged by Pope Gregory, St Augustine made the monastery much more a working establishment, where religious leaders could live alongside monks: clearly the duties of a bishop were incompatible with withdrawal from the world.

Monks and nuns followed the *Rule*. Their basic vows were of obedience, poverty and chastity, and their days were filled with praying, manual labour and reading. With the exception of Sunday, time was spent every day on practical chores such as growing food, building, cleaning, teaching or caring for the sick. Most significantly, at a time when all books had to be produced by hand, they copied books. Monasteries became centres of learning and some built up great and valuable libraries.

Churches and monasteries

Churches and monasteries were the first Saxon buildings made of stone, and examples survive to this day (for example, Brixworth and Earls Barton in Northamptonshire). They must have been objects of great awe and wonder; in a world where most buildings were insubstantial and small, these churches, with their apparent permanence and dominating presence, must have impressed the common people with the power and wealth of the Church. They were a visible and constant reminder of their religion.

Monasteries were generally built on a simple rectangular plan around an open space called the cloister. The sides of the rectangle were occupied by a church for worship, a refectory for dining, and a dormitory for sleeping. There were also working buildings attached for storing and making things, and there would also be a library and visitors' rooms. Monasteries appear to have become very numerous in Saxon times – the diocese of Worcester alone possessed 30 in the middle of the 9th century – and they undoubtedly helped to 'civilize' the barbarous Saxons.

By the middle of the 8th century, York had one of the best libraries in western Europe. These establishments were vital in carrying forward learning and the Christian heritage during a period of turmoil in the western world.

The Venerable Bede

Bede is the most revered and famous monastic figure of the period. From the age of seven, Bede was entrusted to the care of the monks of the Benedictine monastery in Wearmouth (now Tyne and Wear), but before reaching manhood he went to an associated house at Jarrow where some 600 monks lived and worked. Here he had access to a superb library built up by the abbot Benedict Biscop, and he effectively devoted his life to writing, producing so many books that he earned the name *venerable* (or 'highly respected'). His main work was his *History*, which took many years of research and is an indispensable source of information on the Saxon period, without which little would be known of the men and women who peopled these islands at that time. It was written in Latin, the language of the Church, and, of course, is a Saxon Christian view of the period. Bede completed his *History* in 731, four years before his death. He is buried in Durham Cathedral.

Hilda

The period abounds with Saxon and Celtic saints, and St Hilda was one. In 657, St Hilda founded the great monastery for men and women (separated, of course, although the clergy were not celibate at this time) at Whitby. As an Abbess related to the King of Northumbria Hilda wielded considerable influence. She was one of the leaders of the Celtic delegation at the Synod of Whitby, but she accepted the decision of the meeting in favour of Roman rather than Celtic customs. During her life, she became greatly respected and her opinions were sought by leaders of the day.

She encouraged learning and, under her guidance, the monk Caedmon wrote religious poetry in English while at Whitby. (A musical setting of the *Song of Caedmon* is included in the BBC's *Come and Praise* used widely for primary assemblies.) She died in 680 aged 66 years.

St Cuthbert

Cuthbert is one Saxon saint whose origins and life are a little unclear. Born in Ireland, or possibly Northumberland, he became a monk because of a vision he saw as a shepherd boy. He attended the Synod of Whitby and later became Prior of Melrose. Next came a similar appointment at Lindisfarne, but Cuthbert craved solitude. He built himself a hermitage on the Farne Islands. For a few years he reluctantly became a bishop in Hexham and Lindisfarne, but eventually returned to his lonely cell on the Farne Islands where he died. Famous in life, he became even more famous in death, when he was revered and miracles were reported daily at his shrine. The shrine remained in Durham until the Reformation and superstition dictated that no woman was allowed near it.

Why you need to know these facts

Through the people whom the Saxons thought important – saints in particular – we can begin to understand the beliefs and attitudes of the time.

Amazing facts

● Saxon gods gave us some of our day names. Tiw, the god of battles (Tuesday was Tiw's day); Woden, the god of sun, sky and war (Wednesday was Woden's day); Thunor, the maker of thunder and lightning (Thursday is Thunor's day); and Frig, goddess of fertility (Friday was Frig's day).
● Bede had no paper to write on. At this time, only the Chinese knew how to make paper. He wrote on vellum, the cured skin of a calf. Pen ank ink were, like most Saxon utensils, made from naturally occuring materials – quills and fruit dyes.

Teaching ideas

● Examine illuminated manuscript designs. Copy an illuminated letter (you may be able to use a photocopy as a template) and get the children to colour it in.
● Tell the children to investigate the life of a monk. They should draw up a timetable of his day alongside one showing what they would be doing at the same time.
● The Saxons celebrated many saints. Find out about a few of them. Who in the modern world might we elevate to sainthood? Hold a class debate, and see if the children can agree on just two names for this honour – one man and one woman.

Kings and rulers

The myth of Arthur

It is extremely doubtful whether King Arthur was a real person at all, but in the mists of time and the fog caused by lack of evidence on the early Saxon period it is inevitable, perhaps, that an heroic figure such as King Arthur should emerge. He is said to have lived in the 6th century and united the British tribes against the invading Saxons. Although the fame of Arthur is widespread, especially on the Celtic fringes and in Brittany, he is not mentioned in the *Anglo-Saxon Chronicle.* Myths about the Round Table were introduced at the end of the 12th century.

Sutton Hoo

Because evidence about the early Saxon kings is somewhat shaky, the grave goods from the find at Sutton Hoo in Suffolk are particularly significant. It is thought to be the grave of King Raedwald of the East Angles (or one of his successors) who died around 625, although no body has been found at the site. The grave goods are held in the British Museum in London, and are both very revealing and challenging. It is by no means clear what all the objects were used for.

Sutton Hoo is near Woodbridge on the River Deben close to its estuary. In 1938, three low, circular burial mounds were excavated – all had been robbed. When, in 1939, the largest was opened, a magnificent Anglo-Saxon ship burial was discovered containing objects of enormous value. The

finds included a helmet with a realistic face mask, a large shield, a magnificent sword and silver and gold clasps and buckles. Enigmatically, there were Christian objects buried in this pagan-style site. The finds had to be hidden in the London Underground for safety during the Second World War and a thorough examination did not begin until the war was over. The site has been repeatedly excavated, and recent surveys have revealed some twenty low mounds.

The ship, the largest ever found from this period, is about 27 metres long and 4 metres wide. It had been dragged from the River Deben to a hillock 30 metres high, and then placed in a trench and buried. Amidships, a gabled hut, had been built to accommodate a very large coffin and the astonishing grave goods. The finds connect King Raedwald with places as far apart as Sweden and Lombardy, although the strongest connections lie with Sweden.

In only two parts of the world have other ship burials been found: East Suffolk and eastern Sweden. The sword, shield and some other key objects found at the site are also probably Swedish in origin. Many of the objects were locally made, but their design was European. One great silver dish was made in Byzantium; a bronze bowl incised with a camel came from Alexandria in Egypt. Spoons in the grave may have been a christening present.

Although much is speculation, it is clear that connections between Saxon England and the rest of Europe were well established, and that the Dark Ages were not totally devoid of beauty and craftsmanship.

Alfred the Great

King Alfred, King of Wessex, is widely regarded as one of the greatest Saxon kings. He was the youngest son of King Ethelwulf and was born at Wantage in Berkshire in 853 during a very unsettled period. By the time that he had become King of Wessex in 871, most of England north of the Thames was in Viking hands. But even before becoming King he had defeated the Danes in a battle on the Berkshire Downs. These battles to secure his kingdom were to continue. His successes against the Danish leader Guthrum brought a limited period of peace to southern England until fresh Danish raids in the mid-890s. He died around 900 and is buried in Winchester Cathedral.

Alfred was essentially a practical man. His law-making mainly consisted of taking the best practice of previous kings and using it wisely. His writings reveal a man who clearly worked to promote the good of the people and who valued learning highly. His story is closely bound up with that of the Vikings and you will find further information on his exploits in the next chapter.

The stories of great figures in history, in particular Anglo-Saxon kings and rulers, are important because they helped to shape the events of their age, but they are particularly important in this period because so little is known about the Dark Ages.

Why you need to know these facts

*That Alfred established trial by jury, divided England
into counties and founded the University of Oxford.*
He did none of these things. He was perhaps over-lauded by
the Victorians, who gave him the title 'Great'.

● An ambitious project is to work towards a dramatic
reconstruction, perhaps for an assembly, of the Sutton Hoo
burial. You could make replica objects based on pictures of
the real finds, prepare food for the event, and even make up
a ceremony. King Raedwald, the most likely occupant of the
grave, was actually converted to Christianity although the
idea of burial with grave goods is pagan.
● Make a 'Book of Kings'. Find out the names of as many
Saxon leaders as you can and ask the children to write one
entry each.
● Investigate the Alfred Jewel. What was it? Where was it
found? Ask the children to write a story about the jewel that
could be true. The Alfred Jewel can be seen in the
Ashmoleum Museum, Oxford.

Resources

If you live in England there may well be a place worth
visiting nearby (Wareham in Dorset still has its Saxon turf
walls and a Saxon church, St Martins), and you should
certainly investigate the origins of the name of your locality.
Consult *The Concise Oxford Dictionary of English
Placenames* by E Ekwall (Oxford University Press).

The British Museum (020 7636 1555) contains the Sutton
Hoo treasures and the *Anglo-Saxon Chronicle*. Small
collections can be seen elsewhere, particularly:
Wantage Museum, Berkshire (01235 771447) – a small
museum in Alfred's birthplace which contains a copy of the
Alfred Jewel.
The City Museum, Winchester (01962 848269).
The Ashmolean Museum, Oxford (01865 278000) – holds
the Alfred Jewel and also the jewel found at Minster Lovell
near Oxford.
Dorset County Museum, Dorchester (01305 262735).
Devizes Museum, Devizes, Wiltshire (01380 727369).

Books

Translations can be used selectively with children. See:
The Anglo-Saxon Chronicle by G Garmonsway (Dent)
The Battle of Maldon by B Griffiths (Anglo-Saxon Books)
Anglo-Saxon Poetry by S Bradley (Dent) – contains Beowulf
and the Exeter Book riddles.
A beautifully illustrated source is *The Lindisfarne Gospels* by
J Backhouse (Phaidon)
The Sutton Hoo Ship Burial by Angela Care Evans (British
Museum).

Books for chilfdren

The Anglo-Saxons by R Loverance (BBC Fact Finders).
Anglo-Saxon Village by M Stoppleman (A&C Black) –
indispensable book about West Stow.
Family Life in Saxon Britain by Peter Hicks (Wayland) – a
fine book with particularly good illustrations.
Kings, Chiefs and Warriors by Martin Whittock
(Heinemann) – good coverage of the Dark Ages.

Books for teachers

There are many books that are good background reading
for teachers. Those who have the time or the interest might
like to look at *The Anglo-Saxons* edited by James Campbell
(Penguin) – a splendid, detailed, well-illustrated survey.
In search of the Dark Ages by M Wood (Penguin).
The Formation of England by H Finberg (Paladin).

ICT

ICT possibilities should be explored. Try: *Arcventure IV The
Anglo-Saxons* (Sherston); *Saxon Life* (Oak Solutions); Zig
Zag: *The Anglo-Saxons* (Logotron)

Suppliers

PCET is one good supplier of charts for classroom use:
Invaders and Settlers (H104); *The Anglo-Saxons* (E214)

Chapter 7

Invaders and Settlers

The Vikings in Britain

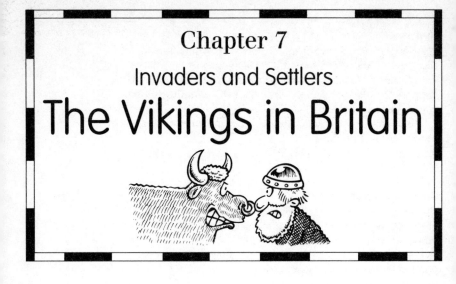

In recent years an increasingly cuddly image has been created of the Vikings. Industrious Viking traders, shopkeepers and craftsmen have been shown to have lived in the thriving town of Jorvik (York), and we now celebrate with confidence Viking journeys across Russia, to the Middle East and to North America. But even though our picture of the Vikings is now more complete, it remains true that they were a fearsome, cruel and heathen people, who extolled warrior virtues and brave death.

The Vikings were one of a number of peoples who invaded and settled in the British Isles in the first millennium AD. This pattern of invasion and settlement largely dictated the unique and different characters of Wales, Scotland, Ireland and England.

Before studying the Vikings in any depth, it is important to understand why this invasion was only one of a number that occurred up to the Norman Conquest in 1066. The section 'Invasion and settlement' on page 66 in Chapter 5 details some of the underlying reasons behind these invasions and applies equally to the invasion by the Vikings.

Who were the Vikings?

The word *Viking* is of uncertain origin but has been applied to all raiders from Scandinavia, whichever land they were from. The raids began in the late 8th century when Vikings sailed to England, Ireland, France (Gaul) and the islands of the north on the easterly winds that prevailed in the spring. But from the 860s Viking groups started to come to England with their families and were prepared to stay. Many historians believe that in this early period there had been a population explosion in the Viking homelands and that there was not enough good farming land to go round.

The Vikings liked the climate of the British Isles and established winter bases in Britain, some of which became permanent. They started to use horses, and conquered and settled further and further from the sea. The ferocity of their raids built up a momentum that seemed unstoppable until, becoming settlers themselves with homes and families to care for, they lost the advantages of mobility and surprise and became vulnerable themselves.

Timeline

Vikings land on the coast of Dorset.	AD789
Vikings sack the monastery at Lindisfarne.	
The Great Army from Denmark invades England.	
King Edmund of East Anglia killed by the Danes.	869
Alfred the Great becomes King of Wessex.	871
Founding of the Danish Kingdom at Jorvik.	
Alfred defeats the Danes.	
Guthrum converts to Christianity.	
Vikings settle in an area of the country that became known as 'Danelaw'.	886
Death of Alfred.	901
Vikings granted lands in Normandy.	911
End of the Viking kingdom of Jorvik.	954
King Harald Bluetooth of Denmark converts to Christianity.	
Vikings make renewed attacks and are bribed with Danegeld.	990
Leif Eriksson lands in North America.	1000
Cnut (Canute) becomes king of England, and later of Denmark and Norway.	1017
Last attack by north-men when Harald Hardrada invades northern England and is defeated by King Harold at the Battle of Stamford Bridge.	1066

Why do we need to know about the Vikings?

Like other invaders before them, the Vikings had a lasting effect upon the places we live in today. Many place names and settlement sites are Viking in origin.

They affected the nature of our government (the Viking *Althing* in Iceland, dating from 902, was Europe's earliest parliament), our traditions and language (phrases such as being 'spread-eagled' and to 'bear witness'; and familiar words like die and skin are Viking legacies).

Knowledge of the first millennium of invasion and settlement in Britain is a National Curriculum requirement.

How do we know about the Vikings?

Evidence of the Viking people comes from a number of sources:
● Sagas (such as the *Vinland Sagas,* written on vellum in the 12th century, 200 years after the events they describe) are an important source, given the lack of written evidence from the Vikings themselves.
● The writings of contemporaries, most of whom were on the receiving end of Viking violence (for example the *Anglo-Saxon Chronicle*). Other writings, such as the *Domesday Book*, also reveal Viking names and habits that were still lingering around at that time in the north of England.
● Archaeological evidence (Jorvik, similar settlements in Scandinavia, and L'Anse Aux Meadows in Newfoundland).
● Place names and settlement patterns.

What happened to the Vikings?

Like other raiders and invaders before them, the Vikings eventually became absorbed with, and indistinguishable from, the other inhabitants of the British Isles. The last true Viking invasion was by the Norwegian, King Harald, who was soundly beaten at the battle of Stamford Bridge by Harold in 1066. But the Normans, who took on the luckless Harold directly after Stamford Bridge and killed him at the Battle of Hastings, were themselves 'north-men' in origin. They had been given part of northern France 150 years previously, following 50 years of repeated attacks.

Norse words and linguistic forms still survive in Britain, particularly in the dialect speech of Yorkshire and Northumberland – in words such as 'lake' and 'play', and in names like Hopkinson and Wilkinson. The Viking language of the Northern Isles, called *Norn*, survived until the 18th century, and the Norwegians had a significant influence on Scottish history until the middle of the 15th century. Norwegian law was not abolished in Shetland until 1611.

Norseman – another name for a Viking.

Longboat – the shallow-drafted ships, pointed at both ends, which carried the Vikings on their raids to Britain.

Prow – the front of the ship; usually adorned with a fierce dragon's head or similar on war vessels.

Danelaw – the area of Britain, north-east of a line marked by the A5, where the Vikings were contained at the time of Alfred.

Danegeld – literally, 'Danish Gold': a bribe, often enormous, paid to the Vikings in order to make them go away. They didn't.

Rune – a letter in the runic alphabet, made from straight lines; these were used to carve inscriptions, usually on stone tablets.

Valhalla – the great palace in the Viking warrior's heaven.

Odin – chief of all the Viking gods, responsible for war and wisdom.

Viking invasion and settlement

Viking raids

Subject facts

The first raid was probably a small skirmish in Dorset, but the best-known early raid was on the monastery at Lindisfarne in 793, which was vividly recorded in the *Anglo-Saxon Chronicle,* and was clearly viewed with horror by the Saxons because of its sacrilegious nature.

The raids on Britain became more and more frequent until, in 851, a Viking army overwintered in England. Over the next few years overwintering became more common, and in 865, so the *Anglo-Saxon Chronicle* tells us, a great army landed in East Anglia and stayed for 14 years whilst being constantly reinforced. The purposes of this army went beyond raiding; it was intent on displacing the Anglo-Saxon kingdoms and their kings. Within 90 years of the first raids, the Vikings had seized Mercia, Northumbria and East Anglia. They consolidated their position in the north by establishing a kingdom based around York that lasted for 80 years, from the mid-870s. The *Chronicle* tells us that the Vikings shared out the land of the Northumbrians and then proceeded to plough it and support themselves. Only Wessex, where Alfred was King, stood in their way.

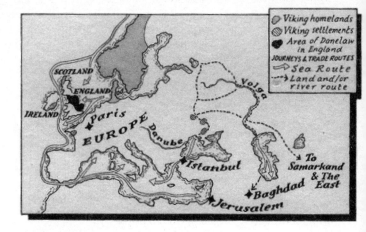

In their own words

On 8th January, the harrying of the heathen miserably destroyed God's church in Lindisfarne by rapine and slaughter.
The Anglo-Saxon Chronicle

They came to the church at Lindisfarne, ravaged and pillaged everything and trampled on the holy places. They killed some of the monks, carried some off in chains and, with insults, chased others naked away. Others they drowned in the sea.
Symeon of Durham, writing 100 years later

Places and names

On the face of it, spotting where the Vikings settled from name endings is easy, yet reading the evidence of the past is never quite so simple. It is worth remembering that names coined by the existing inhabitants were sometimes adapted to suit the pronunciation of the newcomers' own language. The Viking *Jorvik* (meaning 'wild boar creek') was originally the Anglo-Saxon *Eoforwic* (meaning 'wild boar settlement'). The Vikings came to Britain speaking Old Norse, which was similar to the Old English spoken by the Saxons (they would still have heard Celtic spoken by some, as well as Latin in the church).

Many word endings give us a good clue as to the nature of the settlement, but some names are more enigmatic and carry the personal name or nickname. For example, Slingsby from Sleng (idler) and -by (town or farm).

Some common Scandinavian place name endings:

-by – a settlement, including farms and villages
Coningsby	king's village
Ingleby	village of the English
Normanby	village of the Norsemen
Moreby	farm on the moor

-toft – a Danish word originally meaning 'a plot of ground on which a homestead was built'
Brothertoft	Brothir's homestead
Nortoft	North farm
Lowestoft	Hlothver's homestead

-thwaite or **-with** – a clearing in woodland
Tockwith	Toki's wood
Applethwaite	apple-tree clearing
Braithwaite	broad clearing

-thorpe – a small settlement dependent on a larger one
Kettlethorpe	Ketill's hamlet
Copmanthorpe	hamlet of kaupmenn or merchants
Skinnerthorpe	skinner's hamlet

The pattern of Viking settlement supplies evidence as to the nature of the invasion, and helps us understand where they settled and why.

Why you need to know these facts

● On a map of the world, trace journeys made by the Vikings. Ask the children to work out the distances they must have travelled.
● Use an outline map of the United Kingdom to mark places with Scandinavian name-endings. Can the children explain why they appear where they do?
● Eric Thorwaldsson's nickname was Eric the Red and is a typical descriptive Viking name. Other nicknames are Harald Bluetooth, Ragnar Hairy Breeches and Ivar the Boneless. The children will enjoy making up names in the same style.

Teaching ideas

The Vikings and the Anglo-Saxons

It became common for bribes to be paid to the Vikings in order to keep them from attacking the Saxon kingdoms. This was called 'Danegeld'. But bribery was a solution that did not work for long. The Vikings swept all before them and, the *Anglo-Saxon Chronicle* records, in 878 an area of Northumbria was shared out by the Vikings, and then half of the army, led by King Guthrum, moved on to attack Mercia and Wessex.

Guthrum was at first successful and surprised King Alfred of Wessex in his winter quarters at Chippenham. Although Alfred suffered a humiliating defeat and was forced to flee into hiding in the marshes of the Somerset levels, he was in a good position to make a comeback. Alfred's dynasty was well-established, there was no conflict for leadership, and he was manifestly a 'good lord' – one that, in Anglo-Saxon culture, is not easily deserted. His return to defeat Guthrum within months was, nevertheless, astonishing.

The Viking army was very mobile. They used horses to move fast (although they always fought on foot), and had the habit of turning up where the Saxons were not. However, the Viking army was now split and diminished in numbers. Alfred had shown previously that they were not invincible. From a fortified headquarters in the virtually impenetrable Somerset marshes at Athelney, Alfred kept in touch with his loyal lords and built up his forces. After seven weeks of guerrilla warfare, he brought his forces together at Edington, near Westbury in Wiltshire, to face the Danes. He won a complete victory; Guthrum and what was left of his army fled back to Chippenham where, after a fortnight's siege, they were forced by hunger and fear into surrendering. Alfred took hostages and insisted that the leaders of the Danish army should be baptized. He first treated them to a feast and demanded that they promise to leave his kingdom.

Alfred set about securing peace. He made arrangements to ensure that half his army was at home while the other half served in the field. He organized the building of new 60-oared ships for his navy that were swifter and higher than the Vikings'. Most significantly of all, he established 29 fortified *burhs,* or boroughs, so that in Wessex no one was more than 32 kilometres, or a day's march from one.

In 885, the Danes in East Anglia broke the peace and Alfred retaliated by capturing London. After the campaign of 866, a formal treaty established the boundary along

Watling Street of what became known as Danelaw. In this area the rule of law was the rule of the Danes, hence Danelaw. Nearly 30 years later, a Viking army was still unable to penetrate Wessex, largely because of Alfred's burghal system.

King Alfred not only secured his kingdom; he earned a position of leadership recognized by all the English in this island. Furthermore, his was not a passive support of learning – he read and acted on his reading, and we know that he ordered his judges either to learn to read or leave office. He also took the offensive against the Vikings by building ships so that he could match them at sea, and he is sometimes called the founder of the British navy. In spite of modern reassessments of his life, the title King Alfred the Great (not one given in his lifetime) seems likely to stick.

By the 10th century, England was united under one Saxon ruler from the royal house of Wessex, but battles against the Vikings continued. Danegeld became more and more expensive to pay and the Saxons more reluctant to pay it. In 1013 the King of Denmark, Sweyn Forkbeard, made a concerted attempt to conquer Britain and his army overran the Saxons under their leader, Ethelred. When Sweyn died, Cnut (Canute) continued the fight with a fresh Danish army. In 1016 Cnut became the King of all England and Denmark. He sent most of his Danish army back to Denmark and effectively ruled as an English king. This was the height of Viking power in England.

Why you need to know these facts

The Viking confrontation with Alfred marked a change in the nature of the Viking invasions. They truly became settlers, and co-existence and integration began.

Amazing facts

● Norwegian Vikings founded Dublin in 841.
● The Vikings did not only strike westwards from their homelands, they ventured south in to the Mediterranean, and then eastwards to what is known today as Turkey.

Common
misconceptions

While hiding in the marshes in disguise, Alfred was put to watch over some cakes by an old woman. He let them burn and was chastised.
This story appeared over a century after Alfred's death. Of course, the story could have some foundation in fact, but we have no evidence to support it.

Teaching ideas

● As a class, design the front page of a Saxon/Viking newspaper for the day after the battle of Edington.
● Using maps, a gazetteer and any other sources (such as the Internet), ask the children to try to track down the ancient burghs (boroughs) established by Alfred in Wessex.
● Alfred was the only English monarch to have been given the title 'Great'. Do the children think he deserved it? Have a class debate. List all the points for and against his title.

Viking society

Subject facts

Daily life
Excavations, particularly those at Jorvik (York) and Hedeby in Denmark, have thrown considerable light on how Viking urban society operated. Like the Anglo-Saxons, Vikings built their houses of wood, some with walls constructed of wattle and daub, others (at the end of the first millennium) were constructed over pits nearly 2 metres deep and had solid plank walls. The roofs were probably thatched.

Food
The Viking diet was built on a staple of bread, although one visitor to Hedeby noted that 'there was little to eat except fish but there was plenty of it'. Wheat and rye were milled together with some wayside seeds, some of which were poisonous, so there must have had a few dodgy stomachs in the Vikings' lifetime. Other common foods and fruits were eaten in season and considerable use was made of herbs to flavour or to hide flavour. Mead, made from fermented honey and water, provided a strong drink. They reared animals; the majority were slaughtered before the onset of winter because of the difficulty of feeding them during the winter months. Vikings ate hares, deer, fish and horse meat.
  As with all early societies, very little was wasted. Bones were used for brooches, horn for drinking vessels, skins for

clothing. A Viking town had to be self-sufficient: it fired its own pots, made all its own furniture, had its own craftsmen, coin-makers, carpenters, glassblowers and metalworkers.

Clothes

Viking and Saxon men wore similar outfits – trousers and tunics with sleeves. A linen shirt was worn beneath the tunic and a fur or heavy cloth cloak was wrapped around them. They had leather shoes, belts and buckles. Natural dyes made from plants gathered in the countryside produced quite bright colours: blues, purples, greens, yellows and reds. Viking and Saxon women were at first distinguishable because the Vikings wore long pleated dresses with short sleeves, whereas to the Saxon female these were 100 years out of date. They all eventually settled on the loose tunic worn over a long-sleeved dress with their hair covered by a headdress. Amber, jet, silver and gold jewellery was worn extensively by men and women, although gold was rarer and more precious than it is today.

Runes and Sagas

The Vikings had an alphabet, many to be precise, formed from runic letters, which were made up of straight lines. They had no paper, so the runes were mostly carved as inscriptions on stones and memorials, hence the need for straight lines. Although knowing the runes was prized as an almost magical skill, the runic legacy does not form an extensive literature. They are simple records of deeds, memorials to the dead, and sometimes mere graffiti.

The most extensive written record, written long after the events they describe on vellum, were the sagas begun in the 12th century. The Vikings had a strong oral tradition and stories of great deeds were handed down by word of mouth, but eventually came to be written down. The sagas are written in a simple, direct style and are often bloodthirsty. *Njal's Saga*, for example, describes a 50-year blood feud. The *Vinland* (Wineland) *Sagas* tell of Erik the Red's founding of a colony in Greenland and of the discovery of North America by Norsemen 500 years before Columbus.

In their own words

> *Njal's sons had many enemies. Flosi gathered them together and rode to Njal's farm. They surrounded it and set it on fire. When Njal saw there was no escape, he went to bed to die quietly.*
> Njal's Saga

Warriors

Warriors were the most important people in Viking society. At 12 years of age, a Viking boy legally became an adult and would be taken on raids. To be a warrior was the highest ambition. A Viking's weapons were his most precious possessions, and were given names such as Legbiter (a sword), Battle Wall (a shield) and Battle Rain (arrows). Viking warriors wore metal helmets but little other protective armour except leather jerkins. A chief might afford a tunic of chain mail.

Most feared of all the Viking warriors were the berserkers, named after bearskins or bare skins (we are not sure which) which they sported. These warriors fought in a kind of hypnotic rage that may have been drug-induced. They were respected but also feared by other Vikings. Warriors of the great raiding parties that stayed in England were almost certainly professional soldiers who lived from the spoils of war.

Viking society comprised three main groups. At the top were the lords or aristocracy called *jarls*. They were warriors and leaders who were expected to lead by example and not to be outdone by the valour of their men. At the bottom were those in effective slavery, called *thralls*. In the middle of this social sandwich was the largest group, known as *karls*. These included craftsmen, traders and farmers; all the 'middle class' as it were. They were also the warriors who went off to war, leaving their houses and land in the care of the womenfolk.

In their own words

> *Berserkers were men helped by Odin in battle. They refused to wear byrnies and fought like wolves or mad dogs. They began by biting their shield rims, then they cut down the enemy, and neither fire or iron could stop them.*
> Ynglinga Saga

Ships

The Vikings would not have got anywhere without their ships and their famed seafaring ability. Not all Viking ships were the same; it is clear from the substantial finds preserved in the cold water and thick clay of Scandinavia that different ships were built for different purposes. There were cargo ships, merchant ships (called knörr), fishing vessels and longships or warships (often called dragon ships because of the decorated dragon's head that was often carved on the prow). The latter could be up to 55 metres long. The longship preserved in Gokstad in Norway is 23 metres long.

Overlapping planking fastened together with clenched nails (iron rivets) provided the outer skin of the boat, a method of construction called 'clinker'. Gaps between the boards were caulked with moss and tarred wool to make them watertight. At the stern of the ship was the steerboard, used as a crude rudder. A sturdy oak keel provided the ship's backbone, although it was not a true keel, being wider than it was deep. The draught of the ship was shallow, only two to three metres. The bottom of a longship was flat which allowed it to sail in shallow water. It was reasonably light so that it could be dragged over land on wooden rollers. As a result of the advances in ship design Vikings were able to sail further and faster than any before.

A single sail and oars propelled the ships across the North Sea. Each oarsman had his own space, which was called a room. Personal possessions would be kept in a chest on which they sat, but all sorts of general provisions such as water barrels, grain, weapons and even animals were also stored on board.

We cannot understand the Vikings properly without understanding something about the sort of daily lives that the Vikings led.

Why you need to know these facts

● It is thought that berserkers chewed poisonous toadstools (*fly agaric*) to bring on their wild behaviour.

Amazing facts

Vikings wore horned helmets.
This belief has no foundation in evidence, in spite of the fact that Hollywood films have regularly portrayed Vikings in this way. The horned helmet is, rather strangely, used as a symbol of Danish national identity and is worn by crowds at major sporting events such as the Olympic Games or the World Cup.

Common misconceptions

Teaching ideas

● Ask the children to research a runic alphabet and write a short message in runes.

● Make up a story in the style of a saga. It should be told, not written. Try asking some children to retell the story with embellishments. Can they remember it? Could the children sit in a circle and each tell a part of the story made up as they go along? Less confident children could be given prompts of topics by the teacher.

● The Vikings enjoyed using 'kennings': phrases like 'the ship of the ground' to describe a horse. Get the children to create kennings to describe key features of your school (people included). See Literacy hour requirements with regard to kennings.

● Make models of Viking ships. The class could test them using a small fan. Can they design one that will float and sail without toppling?

● The Vikings loved designs with intertwining motifs. Search for as many examples and create a class Viking design book. Use the Internet to gather more information.

● With the children, invent a dance or mime based on the actions of berserkers.

● Using the information gained in the research above, children could give short talks about their lives, or be interviewed for a fictitious (and anachronistic!) radio programme.

● Dress up two children, one male and one female, as citizens of Jorvik as accurately as you can.

● The children could make and decorate (in card) a replica Viking sword based upon archaeological remains extant.

Viking beliefs and deities

Subject facts

People living near the coasts of Britain and Europe were in dread of the Vikings partly because, being heathens, they had no respect for the Church. They were also ferocious warriors because their culture extolled the virtues of a brave death. Ironically, a brave opponent could also be honoured, when captured, by being put to death in an excruciatingly painful way as a celebration of his bravery.

Viking gods were also without mercy and focused on courage and death. Dying in battle was a high honour because you were taken straight to Valhalla (the hall of the chosen or slain), which was a sort of warrior heaven, accompanied by warrior maidens called Valkyries. In this warrior heaven, ruled over by Odin the god of wisdom and war, warriors would fight all day and feast all night. Thor was the god of thunder and justice, and the most popular god with ordinary people – hence the many lucky charms that have been found in the shape of a hammer. The gods Odin and Frey (god of harvest) demanded sacrifices and these could, on occasion, be human.

Viking gods and goddesses belonged to two groups called the Aesir and the Vanir. The Aesir was the larger family; at its head was Odin, the 'all-father'. Odin was the war chief, a sinister god who demanded sacrifice. Victims were slaughtered to ask for victory and to celebrate it. Odin had only one eye – he lost the other in a search for knowledge. He rode on a horse with eight legs and on his shoulders stood two ravens, Hugin (memory) and Munin (mind). They flew into the world to find out what was going on and whispered information in his ears. Odin was a very complicated god and the beliefs that surrounded him were connected with sorcery and evil. Frigg was married to Odin and she was the queen of the Viking gods.

Thor (thunder) rode in a chariot pulled by two goats carrying a hammer, which was the symbol for lightning. Vikings believed that Thor protected them from cold, hunger, giants and many other dangers. He was not clever but was immensely strong, and defended Asgard against any powers that threatened the Viking heaven. The word Thursday comes from his name.

Frey was the third great Norse deity. He belonged to the smaller family of gods, the Vanir, and was the farming god. His wife was Freya was the goddess of love and beauty. She travelled through the sky in a chariot drawn by two cats.

The Vikings and Christianity

Contact with Britain and the rest of Europe brought the Vikings into contact with Christianity, a religion that they were not slow in taking up. Vikings were converted in their homelands and King Harald Bluetooth of Denmark was one of the first to convert in 960. In a typically Viking act, when a Viking king in Kiev became a Christian, he forced all his subjects into the River Dnieper to be baptized. When King Alfred defeated Guthrum, Guthrum too converted to Christianity. But there was a clear period when Christian and pagan beliefs co-existed. A degree of expediency may have accelerated Viking conversions because they were great traders, and most of their trading was carried out across a largely Christian world.

Why you need to know these facts

Although Viking religion was superseded by Christianity, there are still cultural throwbacks to their pagan beliefs lingering in Western society today – the music of Wagner, for example.

Teaching ideas

● Paint pictures to adorn the mythical hall of the dead, Valhalla. Play the *Ride of the Valkyries*, by Wagner, as inspiration.

● Thor's symbol was a hammer. The children could design a lucky charm or brooch that might have been worn by a Viking as a symbol of this god.

● In a class discussion, list all the reasons that the children can think of why the Vikings discarded their gods in favour of the Christian one.

Resources

There are some splendid museums in Scandinavia, but the main (and some smaller museums) in Britain have objects worth viewing. There is clearly some overlap between Saxon and Viking displays, but The Museum of Scotland in Edinburgh, York Museum, Cirencester Museum and The British Museum all hold artefacts. The key site in England is York, and the Jorvik Viking Centre (tel: 01904 643211) produces a valuable information pack for teachers, some excellent slides and a good day out (including smells).

Books
Myths of the Norsemen by Roger Lancelyn Green (Puffin).
Faber Book of Northern Legends by K Crossley-Holland (Faber).
The Viking Saga by H Treece (Puffin).
Viking Mythology by John Grant (The Apple Press).
Scotland's Vikings (HMSO, National Museum of Scotland).
I Was There: Vikings by John Clare (The Bodley Head).
Invaders, the Anglo-Saxons and Vikings Resource Pack (Collins).

The BBC and others produce material from time to time but it is necessary to check what is currently available. *Zig Zag, The Vikings*, was excellent. Contact *Regia Anglorum*, Bristol, (tel: 0117 964 6818) for information on active classroom presentation and hands-on replicas for the period.

Chapter 8

The Aztecs

D o you think of pumping hearts being ripped from human chests by half-naked priests armed with sharp stone knives when you think of the Aztecs? This vivid image may be the one that sticks in the mind, but there was much more to the Aztecs than bloody sacrifice.

Though warlike and callous by our standards, the Aztecs had enormous creative energy and produced well-ordered towns, pyramid temples, palaces and marketplaces – in fact, the most sophisticated civilization that Central America had ever known.

Introducing the Aztecs

Who were the Aztecs?

The name *Aztec* describes the group of people, mainly the Mexica and Acolhua, whose empire dominated Central America in the 15th century AD.

The Valley of Mexico was the heart of the Aztec Empire. It is surrounded by volcanic mountains but has rich deep soil and many shallow salty lakes. An island in the central lake, Lake Texcoco, was the site of the Aztec capital. The rest of central

Mexico is mountainous, with steep wooded slopes, so most people lived in the large highland valleys.

The Aztec Empire lasted from 1428 to 1521. This is the classic Aztec period when their culture flourished and dominated Central America. But the roots of the Aztec civilization go back much further to the nomadic Mexica tribe living in the northern desert. These Nahuatl-speaking people migrated south around AD1150, and over the next 200 years a series of city-states were founded.

Once the Mexica had settled in these areas where there were abundant and rich food supplies, the population grew rapidly. Swamp delicacies (cakes made out of algae, fish, turtles, salt and insect larvae) were exchanged for building materials and other desirable commodities. The Aztecs were fierce warriors so they gradually became both rich and powerful. Their domination was finally asserted in a series of alliances and conquests.

The map below shows Southern Mexico and the Central American states today. The shaded area shows the extent of the Aztec Empire just before its collapse in 1521. Archaeologists refer to this area as *Mesoamerica*.

Timeline

CAD1150	*Migration of the nomadic Mexica tribe southwards to Central America.*
c1200	*Nomadic Aztec tribe reaches the Valley of Mexico claiming to be descendants of the warlike Toltecs.*

Aztecs establish their great city of Tenochtitlan on a swampy island in Lake Texcoco.	c1325
The 'Triple Alliance Empire' – the height of Aztec civilization.	1428–1519
Spanish military leader Hernán Cortés sets sail from Cuba with an army of 500 and 11 ships to explore the coast of Mexico. On landing in Mexico, Cortés is greeted by messengers from the Aztec king, Moctezuma II.	Feb 1519
Cortés enters Tenochtitlan.	Nov 1519
Fighting breaks out in the capital between the Spanish and the Aztecs.	
Moctezuma dies, possibly killed by a stone thrown by one of his own people.	
Noche triste (the night of sorrows). The Spanish fight their way out of the capital taking many casualties.	June 30th 1520
Fall of Tenochtitlan, the Aztec capital, to the combined forces of the Spanish, and the Cholollan and Tlaxcalan Indians. End of the Aztec Empire.	1521
Typhus and other diseases kill 60 per cent of the Aztec population.	1521–1548

After the conquest, Spanish gradually replaced Nahuatl as the main language spoken, and by the beginning of the 20th century most, if not all, Mexicans were of partial Spanish ancestry.

Why do we need to know about the Aztecs?

The Aztecs established the largest and most remarkable empire in Mesoamerican history and their creative achievements, particularly in civic organization, are impressive. But the fall of the Aztec Empire marked a major turning point in American history and permanently changed the culture of the region. Pre-Hispanic heritage still profoundly affects Mexico, and is critically important to our understanding of modern America.

The Aztecs is one of the world history options for Key Stage 2 history in the National Curriculum, and generally a very popular one.

How do we know about the Aztecs?

Native pictorial manuscripts provide a limited amount of information. The Aztec pictorial writing system could not record the spoken word fully, only a limited range of names and ideas. These 'pictures' were used to jog the memory of the reader who would then fill in the detail from his own knowledge. The manuscripts (called codices) were written on paper made from the inner bark of the wild fig tree or deerskin. Only a few survive from before the Spanish conquest, although they continued to be painted for generations after the end of the Empire.

Several of the conquerors wrote reports of their deeds. Cortés himself and Diaz del Castillo wrote at length, but they give an account from the Spanish viewpoint only.

The years following the conquest were extensively chronicled by Spanish priests (Friar Diego Duran and Friar Bernardino de Sahagun made systematic records of Aztec culture). Ixtlilxochitl and Chimalpahin wrote two particularly important chronicles; both writers were descendants of Aztec nobles.

Archaeology, especially when aided by modern technology, continues to yield information about the Aztec past. Many Aztec sites lie under Mexico City.

What happened to the Aztecs?

The end of the Aztec Empire was precipitated by a Spanish invasion in 1521. Attracted by tales of an amazing civilization, rich beyond measure, and fired by religious conviction that is hard for some to understand today, an army of Spanish adventurers (usually referred to as conquistadores) under Hernán Cortés set out to explore the region. They were welcomed at first, albeit warily, by the Aztecs, and invited into the capital Tenochtitlan by Moctezuma, the emperor.

The Spanish were in Tenochtitlan for two weeks as guests, but they soon realized that they were virtual prisoners. They seized Moctezuma as a hostage and held him for several months, but the city began to seethe with unrest. The emperor tried appeasement, and even built a Christian shrine on the steps of the great pyramid as a concession to the Spaniards. Moctezuma warned Cortés that he could not control his people and told the Spanish to leave for their own safety. The Spaniards killed some Aztec lords and the Aztecs attacked, seeking vengeance; the emperor was called upon to calm his people but, according to Spanish accounts, he was stoned by them and died. Native historians later claimed that the Spanish strangled him. The truth is uncertain.

After being forced to beat a hasty retreat from Tenochtitlan at night and with many casualties, the small Spanish army, combined with thousands of opportunist Cholollan and Tlaxcalan Indians, returned to lay siege to the city.

Superior tactics and weapons (the Aztecs had no firearms), combined with the decimating effect of starvation, disease and the lack of fresh water, eventually led to the fall of the city in August 1521. During the final attack, wholesale slaughter was carried out by the Tlaxcalans on their former oppressors with a ferocity that shocked even the battle-hardened Spanish. In the confusion, the last emperor, Cuauhtemoc, was captured as he tried to escape. His surrender was accepted by Cortés himself who treated him honourably. A quarter of a million Aztecs in Tenochtitlan were overcome by a force of no more than 900 Spaniards and several thousand Indian allies.

Having defeated the Aztecs, the Spanish set about systematically converting the Indian population to Christianity. Spanish priests arrived who learned the Nahuatl language to speed up the conversion process; they sometimes carried out mass baptisms. Aztec temples were razed to the ground and Christian churches were built on top of some of the largest pyramids. Alongside this religious conversion, a feudal system of tribute and labour was used to control the conquered. But more significantly and dramatically, the native population was also reduced by disease to little more than a tenth of its former size within forty years (the best estimate of Aztec numbers in the years immediately preceding the conquest is 920 000). The Spanish stripped the country of its gold and silver, melted down the sacred objects and shipped most of the treasure back to Spain. (Divers still retrieve treasure from the ships that sank en route to Europe.)

In their own words

> *Like monkeys they seized upon the gold. For in truth they thirsted mightily for gold; they stuffed themselves with it, and starved and lusted for it like pigs.*

The words of a native observer describing Spanish reaction to the gifts offered to them by Aztec ambassadors.

● Nahuatl is one of 50 languages still spoken in Mexico today.
● A series of epidemics – chiefly measles, typhus and smallpox – wiped out most of the Aztecs. These diseases were brought to the new world by Spanish conquistadores and the native population had no resistance to them. The biggest killer was typhus, which killed an estimated 60 per cent of the Aztec population in the period between 1545 and 1548.

Amazing facts

Vocabulary

Codice – a manuscript of 'glyph' writing.
Chinampa – a raised field created in a swampy area for agriculture.
Nahuatl – the language spoken by the majority of Aztecs.
Obsidian – very hard stone (black volcanic glass) used for cutting and weaponry.
Pochteca – professional merchants in the Aztec markets.
Texcoco – the lake and swamp where the capital Tenochtitlan was built.
Tlachtli – an Aztec ballgame.

Aztec society

Subject facts

The soil really was the Aztec lifeblood, and their lives revolved around the demands of farming – planting, weeding, winnowing and storing grain. The soil was used to sustain life and also to give pleasure – the rich created wonderful gardens that greatly impressed the first Europeans to see them.

Diet
The Aztec diet was basically vegetarian with animal supplements – maize was eaten in large quantities. Meat from hunted animals formed a minor part of the Aztec diet, which was supplemented by beans, the prickly pear cactus, and the widespread consumption of insects including ants, grasshoppers, maguey worms and jamil bugs. Chillis provided Vitamin C, and they ate squashes, calabashes, tomatoes and sweet potatoes. Maguey and cotton were grown to provide fibre for weaving.

Social structure
Aztec society was divided into nobles and commoners, and there was a wide gap between them. Although the nobles were greatly outnumbered, they owned most of the land, commanded the army, and lived lives of luxury. Commoners owed some duties to both kings and nobles but managed to live much of their lives without undue interference. The nobles both lived and worked in their large palaces.

Growing up
Between the ages of 10 and 20 all boys and girls attended schools. They received training in singing, dancing and

playing musical instruments. Boys were taught separately from girls and the main elements in their curriculum were martial arts and military training. Children of promising commoners were taught the arts and military, religious and astrological knowledge, alongside the children of nobles in special schools.

Men married in their early twenties and girls were often married as early as 10 or 12 years of age.

The arts

Amongst other activities the Aztecs derived pleasure from dancing and singing. Most of this was done at ritual and ceremonial occasions – we do the same at weddings and birthdays. The dances were rhythmically strong and involved chanting. Some were sober and formal, but the 'dances of youth' were flirtatious and exciting. Spanish priests thought that the Aztec 'wriggling and face pulling' in these dances was highly improper and immoral.

Pottery flutes, rattles and trumpets made from cut conch shells were used in music-making, as were wooden gongs. Feather bundles and rattles featured in most dances.

Skill in performing hymns and poetry was greatly admired, as was public oratory – perhaps not surprising in a culture that lacked a subtle written language.

Stone was a major medium for sculpture and animals were the most frequent subject, particularly snakes and the highly important jaguar. The jaguar was a symbol of power and strength and carvers produced many small ritual objects of this sort. Art, as in all early societies, was functional – the concept of 'art for art's sake' was unheard of. Painting used ritual symbols such as a feathered serpent and standardized geometric images. Strong black outlines were combined with bright flat colours and exaggerated main features to produce a clear distinctive style.

Aztec hieroglyphs

Aztec picture-writing was a bit like modern logos or coats of arms, in that the signs and symbols always told a story.

In their own words

There are very refreshing gardens with many trees and sweet-scented flowers and bathing places of fresh water. Within the orchard is a great pool of fresh water with sides of handsome masonry and a well-laid pavement of tiles. The pool contains many different kinds of fish and waterfowl. There are hedges of latticework made of cane behind which are plantations of all sorts of trees and aromatic herbs.
Hernán Cortés

Why you need to know these facts

Knowledge about the quality of life in Aztec times is necessary in order to understand why many consider the Aztecs to have been 'civilized'. Blood sacrifices need to be seen against a backdrop of an organized and impressive culture.

Amazing facts

● Cornflakes are made from maize, which was a staple of the Aztec diet. Do you start the day the Aztec way?
● The Aztecs did not use money. Most trade was by barter, but cacao beans were used as a kind of currency.
● The Aztecs chewed gum (chicle and bitumen) to clean their teeth.

Common misconceptions

The Aztecs were cannibals.
Strictly not true. Although human flesh was sometimes consumed by warriors as part of religious ceremonies, the Aztecs did not eat human beings as part of their staple diet.

Teaching ideas

● Examine some familiar modern 'glyphs' such as the badge of Arsenal Football Club or your county or city coat of arms. Explain what the pictures mean.
● Create an Aztec-type hieroglyph to represent your school, home, street or village.
● Investigate Aztec art by choosing an example to copy. There is a famous turquoise mosaic mask in the British Museum that you could reconstruct using a clay or

Plasticine base. Smear Vaseline over the carefully shaped head and cover with strips of paper. Complete the mask with coloured paper and PVA adhesive. Add an extra layer of PVA for a glossy effect, and separate from the clay base.

Religion

The central idea of Aztec religion was that of *sacrifice*. The Aztecs believed in many gods who sacrificed themselves for the benefit of mankind: in one myth the gods threw themselves on a huge fire to create the sun.

Creation myth

Creation myths are common to most religions and the Aztec religion is no exception. In the beginning there was a high god called Ometeotl (the name means 'two-god' because there was both male and female in him). This 'two-god' produced four sons who were given the task of creating people, the earth and other gods. They began the cyclical pattern of creation and destruction that formed the religious frame to Aztec lives.

The birth of the sun was a critical occasion because it provided the logic that supported the Aztec practice of human sacrifice: two gods jumped into a fire to create the sun. The first sun that appeared (our moon) worried the gods because it might be too bright, so they threw a rabbit at it to dim it (a shape that can sometimes be seen on its surface today). But it did not move. The second sun could only be made to move by more sacrifice, so the remaining gods removed their hearts and sacrificed themselves to make the sun move across the sky.

And thus, just as the gods sacrificed themselves for the sun, so the Aztecs believed that people also had to provide blood and hearts to keep the sun going.

Some of this blood the Aztecs provided by personal bloodletting as part of worship (generally body piercing by thorns through ears, tongues and genitals), but most was by human sacrifice. Those sacrificed were nearly always prisoners captured in battle, which explains why there was such a constant need for wars. This in turn accelerated the expansion of the Aztec Empire and explains why people eventually turned so violently against the Aztecs when they were given the chance to side with the invading Spaniards.

Sacrificial knives

The sacrificial knives were made of obsidian. Obsidian is a black volcanic glass occurring naturally in Central America. It is rather brittle and when split produces extremely sharp edges – sharper than any known tool, ancient or modern. A well-knapped edge can be sharper than a surgeon's scalpel.

Time

The Aztecs believed that time was divided into a number of ages of existence (we are currently in the fifth age which is due to end in 2027), each presided over by a different sun, controlled by a different god, and peopled by a different race. Each age was believed to end in a violent catastrophe.

In their own words

> *Four men stretched the captive out on the sacrificial stone grasping his arms and legs. In the hand of the fire priest lay the knife. When he had split open his breast, he at once seized the heart. And he whose breast he laid open was quite alive... The bodies were rolled down the steps of the temple, and the steps were bathed in blood.*
> From an account told to Friar Sahagun

Why you need to know these facts

Unless we understand the logic behind the bloody religious practices of the Aztecs we may fall into the error of thinking that what they did was simply due to bloodlust or, worse, that they were just stupid. One cannot understand the Aztecs without understanding their religion. They were no less intelligent than us, but as to whether they were as civilized will depend upon your definition of the word.

Amazing facts

● The hearts of prisoners were removed whilst they were still alive. Their heads were cut off for mounting on skull racks that were next to the pyramid.
● A Spanish witness has calculated that the skull rack by the Great Temple could hold over 1 000 000 heads.

Common misconceptions

The Aztecs thought that the Spanish invaders might be gods.
This is most unlikely. Although it was believed that Moctezuma (the Aztec emperor at the time of the Spanish arrival) 'trembled on his throne in the mountains' at the

thought of meeting the supernatural Cortés, modern
research suggests that this was a rewriting of the events by
Aztec historians seeking to explain the sudden end of the
Aztec Empire.

● When teaching the Aztecs, choose a few questions to
answer. You cannot teach everything, so be selective. Make
sure you take the opportunity to discuss the Spanish–Aztec
culture clash. Although the Spanish admired Aztec
achievements, they regarded them as heathens and had no
sympathy with their religious practices. However, they did
not indulge in ethnic cleansing as is sometimes assumed.
● Imagine that you are an Aztec commoner. Explain to a
foreign visitor why so many people have to be killed on the
steps of the temple.

Tenochtitlan and Aztec cities

There was no place in the world like the Aztec capital
Tenochtitlan; it was unique in size and design. It was a
working city built to impress both people and gods and to
intimidate enemies. When the Spanish first caught sight of it
they were amazed. This was partly because of its size: it was
the largest city ever built in the ancient New World and,
with nearly a quarter of a million inhabitants, it was larger
than any European city at the time.

As the Spanish approached the city along the long
straight causeways, crossing the drawbridges constantly
being raised and lowered to let through the trading canoes
and flat-bottomed barges, one can imagine their
astonishment. Alongside them, as they entered, ran large
aqueducts bringing fresh water to the inhabitants.

The city of Tenochtitlan was carefully laid out in a
regular grid pattern, with four major avenues which divided
it into segments originating from the sacred precinct (see
page 122). The most important axis was east to west – the
route of the sun – and the canals and roads ran at right
angles in order that everything followed the same
orientation. Small flat-roofed houses clustered together in
places, although farmers still coexisted in the city on more
spacious plots of firm land. Along the canals and roads the
traders plied their wares; most of the heavier loads were
transported by water.

In the other city-states in central Mexico, the majority of the housing was well spaced out and interspersed with gardens and fields. Houses were not laid out in a formal plan and generally were simple structures built of adobe bricks (unfired bricks that were simply dried in the sun).

City centre

At the heart of Aztec cities was an open public square bordered by religious and administrative buildings. Tenochtitlan was again unique, for at its heart was a sacred central walled precinct to which public access was limited. It was square, about 500 metres (1640 feet) across, and packed with temples, altars, shrines, schools and assembly halls. But all this was dominated by the towering twin stairway of the pyramid-temple.

Chinampas

Surrounding Tenochtitlan were fertile fields called *chinampas*, created in the swampy lake areas. Long straight ditches drained away the excess water to form artificial islands edged with trees to hold the soil in place. Farmers would have been seen canoeing from field to field.

Town and country

When the Spanish first came to Mexico, it was a fairly stable, safe place for the Aztecs, because they dominated the surrounding peoples. The countryside was safe enough to live and work in, so cities were largely places for merchant and workshop activity, not walled defensive retreats as was often the case in Europe. They were quite rural in appearance and there was no sharp division between countryside and town.

Few cities had a population of more than 20 000; the average administrative capitals in the Valley of Mexico had around 9000 inhabitants. The smallest cities deserving of the name had around 800 residents but had considerable space given over to farming. Peasants who were relatively prosperous and not like medieval serfs in Europe came to the cities daily to attend the markets, to pay taxes and to take part in religious and other festivals.

An open square was at the heart of the city, with the king's palace, a temple and other civic structures arranged on the four sides. The temple was always sited on the east side. A stairway led up the west front of the temple-pyramid to a platform and the roofed temple rooms that always crowned the structure. In the city square there was often a court for playing the game of *tlachtli*.

Tlachtli

We do not have an equivalent of the Aztec ballgame *tlachtli*, because it involved religion, ritual, entertainment, gambling and athleticism. It was kind of tennis played with a hard rubber ball on a court in the shape of a capital 'I'. Without rackets, players (individuals and teams) attempted to put the ball through carved stone rings placed vertically on the central walls. They could only use their hips or knees, and they wore protective clothes made of deerskin. A goal finished the game, but these were apparently rare and points usually decided the issue. These were awarded for particular manoeuvres or skills. The game could last a long time and the winner might be awarded prizes of feathers or even the clothes of the spectators. Games were sacred events that the priests used as omens for the future. Feathers and jade were gambled on the outcome but it was not unknown for farms, children and even personal freedom to be staked.

In their own words

> *On seeing the ball come at them, as it was about to touch the floor, the players were so quick to turn their knees or buttocks to the ball they returned it with extraordinary swiftness. With this bouncing back and forth they suffered terrible injuries on their knees and thighs.*
> Diego Durán, a Spanish priest writing about the game

The marketplace

Every city had its market, but the largest in the ancient world was the one in Tlatelolco, which was Tenochtitlan's twin city, and part of the large conurbation now covered by Mexico City. The marketplace was well-organized, and policed by up to a dozen judges who held court in a fine building on the edge of the market square. Cheats and thieves could be executed; officials patrolled the stalls checking on the sales. Each type of merchandise had its own particular place in the market and everything was sold by number and measure, but not by weight. Slaves, medicines, and dogs for eating could be purchased. You could also have your hair cut or buy a fish pie. Most city markets took place once a week but the largest of all opened every day. Amongst goods spotted by a Spanish observer were stone knives, brass axes, rabbits, honey, sandals, rope, lion, otter, jackal, deer, cotton, henequen, (a plant grown for its leaf fibres), salt, beans, herbs, fruit, tripe, maize and cochineal.

The jewel in the crown of Aztec civilization was its city-states, and to understand the Aztecs you must understand this achievement. To understand the significance of Tenochtitlan, for example, you need to grasp the fact that it would have ranked as one of the wonders of the world at that time, and that it exceeded every city in Europe in both size and sophistication.

In their own words

> *Proud of itself is the city of Mexico-Tenochtitlan.*
> *Here no one fears to die in war.*
> *This is our glory.*
> *This is your command, oh Giver of Life!*
> *Have this in mind, oh princes do not forget it.*
> *Who could conquer Tenochtitlan?*
> *Who could shake the foundation of heaven?*
> Aztec poem

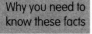

Why you need to know these facts

Aztec cities overwhelmed the Spanish with their beauty and grandeur when they first came upon them. You cannot understand the Aztec achievement without understanding their cities.

Amazing facts

● There were no wheeled vehicles or beasts of burden in ancient Mexico; everything was transported by boat or carried by porters.
● There were no weighing scales in an Aztec market. Goods were sold only by number.
● Tenochtitlan means 'Among the stone-cactus fruit.'

Teaching ideas

● Build a model of the heart of the Aztec capital. Make sure that it is correctly orientated. Research the project properly before you begin.
● Create a game like *tlachtli*. Mark out a court and make up the kind of rules that the Aztecs must have had. Don't be frightened of changing rules to make the game more fun.
● Collect and display (correctly labelled) goods (pictures will do) that could be bought in an Aztec market.
● Act out a scene in the market court where a trader is accused of giving short measure.

Military skills were highly prized by the Aztecs. A council of four noblemen ran the army. Warriors, who had earned their position by skill and courage, formed the officer's corps. To enter the highest order of officers you had to have performed at least 20 deeds of bravery and captured many prisoners. Special headdresses, jewellery and clothing marked out each rank, such as eagle and jaguar warriors.

Ordinary soldiers

The common soldier wore war suits of animal skins while the nobles had suits woven from feathers that were highly prized. The great mass of infantry wore body paint for identification and fought barefoot. They were armed with stabbing javelins, obsidian-bladed clubs and round leather-trimmed shields. There was no standing army and men were called up for specific campaigns, the smallest units being led by their own community leaders.

The reason for wars

The main object of battle was to capture prisoners, so the Aztecs had no concept of fighting to the finish. Had they done so, the Spanish would not have escaped from Tenochtitlan after the death of Moctezuma. Battle was an extension of religious practice; indeed, warriors ritually ate flesh taken from the thighs of sacrificed captives. The conquistadores found this beyond their understanding and this kind of cultural miscomprehension contributed to the final and fatal conflict with the Aztecs.

Aztec society was built on military strength. Military skill was needed to subjugate the surrounding tribes and to sustain their religion. Military failure was the occasion of the fall of the Empire.

● Moctezuma sent emissaries to greet Cortés carrying many presents. The Spaniards rejected what the Aztecs regarded as the most significant of their gifts – food (tortillas, turkeys, eggs, guavas and so on) sprinkled with the blood of sacrificed humans.

● Make an inventory of Aztec weapons with illustrations and descriptions.
● The main aim of warfare was to take prisoners, not to kill. Debate how this might have helped the Spanish to defeat the Aztecs even though they were greatly outnumbered.

Resources

The number of books about the Aztecs has increased since the topic was included in the National Curriculum. The following are a sample of useful books now available:
Aztec Times by Antony Mason (Marshall Publishing).
Explorers by Dinah Starkey (Collins).
Art from the Past, The Aztecs by Gillian Chapman (Heinemann).
Mexican Pictorial Manuscripts (The Bodleian Library, Oxford).
The Aztecs by Richard F Townsend (Thames and Hudson).
The Aztecs by Michael E Smith (Blackwell).

Look in journals such as *Junior Education* (for example April 1999), *Primary History* (Historical Association), for occasional articles and teaching materials.

Other resources
High street food shops can provide a different resource worth exploring (tortillas, guacamole etc) and you may also find travel agents useful. There are specialists who will run workshops for schools on Mexican culture and history eg *Quetzal*, Mexican Arts and Crafts, 61 New Road, Chippenham SN15 1ES, (tel: 01249 652496).
The British Museum, London (tel: 020 7636 1555) – since the closure of the Museum of Mankind in 1997, the main Aztec exhibits have been held in The British Museum. A new Mexican Gallery has been opened and the collection is slowly being enlarged.
University Museum of Natural History – The Pitt Rivers Collection, Oxford 01865 270927.
Cadbury's World, Bourneville, Birmingham (tel: 0121 451 4180) – a surprising venue, but there is an interesting display about cocoa that has fascinating and worthwhile material on the Aztecs.

Chapter 9
Britain and the wider world in Tudor times

The Tudor period was a time of powerful rulers, memorable heroes and heroines, and of a growing awareness of the wider world. England was generally more wealthy, more powerful and peaceful than ever before. It was also an age of sea exploration, when new trade routes were established and new lands were discovered.

We remember the Tudors for their great literature, for the resonant phrases of Shakespeare and the Prayer Book, and for the works of Marlowe and Spencer. We remember too, religious turmoil when the Church of England was separated from Rome, the monasteries were dissolved, and Catholics and Protestants were both cruelly persecuted in their turn.

Introducing the Tudors

Who were the Tudors?

Subject facts

The Tudor period (1485–1603) and dynasty began when Henry Tudor defeated Richard III at the battle of Bosworth. The year 1485 marked the end of the Wars of the Roses and the beginning of a dynasty that was to last until the death of Elizabeth I in 1603. Henry's grandfather was Welsh and it was his name, *Tewdwr,* that was subsequently treated as a surname by the English.

In Tudor times there was no United Kingdom. Although England and Wales were joined by an Act of Union in 1536, Scotland was a separate kingdom against which the English fought. At the battle of Flodden in 1513, Scotland lost its king, James IV, and the cream of its nobility. In Ireland, attempts to Anglicize the Gaelic Irish largely failed but, in spite of this, Henry VIII called himself 'King of Ireland'.

For most of the Tudor period, the English not only ruled England, but part of France as well. (Until the 1430s England had suzerainty over Bordeaux, and a large area of land to the south of it and most of the area to the north of the Loire.) But by 1453, the English had been expelled from everywhere except Calais.

Timeline

AD1485	*Battle of Bosworth – Henry Tudor defeats Richard III and becomes Henry VII.*
1492	*Christopher Columbus discovers America.*
	Henry VIII becomes king.
1511	*Launch of the* Mary Rose.
1513	*Battle of Flodden between England and Scotland. James IV of Scotland killed.*
1519	*Magellan began first circumnavigation of the world.*
1520	*Field of Cloth of Gold (a meeting between Henry VIII and Francis I of France where a great deal of wealth was on display).*
1535	*Dissolution of the monasteries.*
1536	*England and Wales joined by the Act of Union.*
1539	*Great Bible published in English. Sinking of the* Mary Rose.
1547	*Edward VI becomes king.*
1553	*Mary I becomes queen.*
1558	*Elizabeth I becomes queen.*
1565	*Hawkins introduced sweet potatoes and tobacco to England.*
1576	*The* Theatre *opens in Shoreditch.*
1577–1580	*Sir Francis Drake's voyage around the world.*
1587	*Drake attacks Cadiz – 'singes the King of Spain's beard'.*
1588	*Defeat of the Spanish Armada.*
1603	*Elizabeth I dies; crown passes to James VI of Scotland.*

Why do we need to know about the Tudors?

The Tudor dynasty lasted for just over a century, and during that time England grew economically, militarily and culturally. It managed to keep its independence from its more powerful European neighbours, France and Spain; the foundations of today's predominantly protestant England were laid and, with the Act of Union, so were the foundations of the present United Kingdom.

How do we know about the Tudors?

English is the key to evidence about the Tudors. It was in this period that official documents gradually moved from Latin to English, so we not only have ready access to colloquial sources in English, but to official ones too. Although, even in English, Tudor documents can be hard to read, it does mean that children can begin to tackle original documents for the first time. The Tudor age is also the first period in British history from which common domestic architecture begins to survive, although only houses of the better sort are still standing from the 16th century.

Vocabulary

Circumnavigation – to journey around (usually to sail around the world).
Colony – a group of people who have made new homes in a foreign country.
Indigenous – earliest known inhabitants of a country.
Empire – a collection of countries and peoples ruled by one person or state.
Scurvy – a disease caused by the lack of Vitamin C that causes bleeding under the skin, anaemia, and spongy gums. Suffered by sailors on long journeys without fruit or vegetables.
Annul – to cancel, especially the legality of a marriage.
Dissolution – the deliberate breaking up of the monasteries and the seizing of their wealth by Henry VIII.
Progresses – Elizabeth journeyed around her kingdom every summer in order to be seen by as many people as possible. These were known as *progresses.*

Elizabethan society

Town and country

Subject facts

Daily life was really country life for everybody, unless you happened to live in London, which was the only really urban area. Even Londoners were not far from the countryside. England was relatively undeveloped, a green agricultural land with many deep forests and a population of around 2 million at the start of the period. However, 100 years later the population of England had almost doubled, but the country still produced enough food to support its people. As the land-owning classes became richer, the poor tended to become poorer. Displaced rural peasants wandered the country as vagabonds.

Sickness and health

Life expectancy was about 38 years; plagues and periodic epidemics affected the size of population, especially in towns, and poor sewage disposal aggravated the problem. On the whole doctors were not much use to the sick, with the practice of bleeding exacerbating rather than aiding recovery. In any case, most people did not have access to doctors but used local traditional treatments. There was no protection against big killers such as diphtheria or measles, and even a simple fracture could lead to amputation, gangrene and death.

Dress

There was no single Tudor style, and fashions changed just as they do today, although fashion was really only something that concerned the rich – the poor could not afford to be fussy about what they wore. One significant feature of much of the Tudor period, especially during the reign of Henry VIII, was that men were just as brightly dressed as women, if not more so. Men wore hose, similar to modern tights, and a frequently used technique was to slash the sleeves and bodice of the top jacket in order to reveal brightly coloured shirts beneath.

Education

Queen Elizabeth was well educated, but she was a daughter of the aristocracy. Education was not generally thought to be necessary for girls. People who could afford it (like Shakespeare's parents) sent their sons to school. At least 135 free grammar schools were started during the reign of Elizabeth, although they charged most pupils. Latin, logic and religion were the staple diet of subjects, and the children were force-fed their lessons if necessary by the use of harsh discipline.

Houses

The houses of the poor have vanished. They were poorly constructed hovels and have not stood the test of time. People lived in simple, usually thatched, cottages on an earthen floor. Most of their daily needs were provided locally and they were never far from a source of water. Life continued largely as it had done for centuries, with an annual timetable dictated by the seasons, the weather, and Holy Days. The Parish Church was often the centre of village life and the parson (the *person*) might well be the only man who could read and write in the community. The church bell summoned people to church, attendance at which was compulsory, and it was also used to warn of danger. Bells were rung when the Armada approached.

What we commonly regard as Tudor houses, especially the black and white half-timbered variety, were largely the substantial dwellings of wealthy yeoman farmers. Many of these have survived. There was a great increase in this type of house-building as agriculture flourished in the 1560–70s.

Large mansions now ceased to be fortified (the country experienced almost unbroken internal peace during the reign of the Tudor monarchs) and were more comfortable than previously. Glass-producing techniques improved and more and more glass windows began to appear. A feature of large houses was often a long gallery, which was used for games, dancing, fencing and simply walking. More fireplaces were constructed and extravagant Tudor chimneys became an ostentatious outward show of an owner's wealth. Hardwick Hall, Compton Wynyates and Hampton Court are fine examples of great Tudor mansions.

To understand the lives of men and women in Tudor times, we must look beyond political events and the stories of great men and women to see how everyday people coped with everyday priorities.

Why you need to know these facts

Tudor houses were all 'black and white half-timbered'. Houses were built of local materials because of the difficulty of transporting heavy materials over long distances. Some were built entirely of stone, and even brick buildings began to be more common. Half-timbered houses were most common in the south and east and places like Cheshire and Herefordshire. The black and white painted appearance is largely a modern affectation.

Common misconceptions

● Design and build a model of the timber framework of a Tudor house. You might use centimetre squared cross-section dowels as the main model building material.
● Weave wattle. (I don't advise making daub: cow dung. Even if it is readily available in your classroom, it might get up an inspector's nose.)
● Map a suitable (if you have one) local area or street. Walk the ground and mark on all Tudor buildings and 'mock' Tudor references. How can you tell mock from real?
● Write an estate agent's guide to a Tudor house.

Tudor monarchs

Subject facts

Henry VII (1485–1509)

Defeated Richard III at Bosworth and ended the Wars of the Roses. By strong, as well as diplomatic, action he brought his rich and powerful subjects to heel and stopped the medieval warring that had troubled the country. His wife, Elizabeth of York, is the figure that has been used on playing cards for the last 500 years – they were invented during his reign.

Henry VIII (1509–1547)

Second son of Henry VII. Although he was talented (he was the first English king to write, publish and print a book), his ambitions to rule France, to dominate the Church, and to produce a son and heir, caused much anguish in his reign. He could not stand being thwarted. When the Church opposed him over his wish to divorce and remarry, he dispensed with Cardinal Wolsey (who died en route to his trial) and established himself as the head of the Church of England. He then dissolved the monasteries and seized their wealth. Henry built up a strong navy but ruled without a standing army.

Edward VI (1547–1553)

Son of Henry VIII and his third wife, Jane Seymour, Edward ruled from the age of nine until his death aged 15. Without a strong adult ruler, the country began to drift into faction. Nevertheless, the pious Edward accelerated England's move towards Protestantism. His reign saw the introduction of the *Book of Common Prayer* (compiled by Thomas Cranmer), and greater uniformity of worship.

Mary I (1553–1558)

England's first woman ruler, daughter of Henry VIII and his first wife Catherine of Aragon, hers was not a happy reign. Her Catholic fervour and intolerance led to some 300 people being burned at the stake for their religious beliefs, including the bishops Latimer, Ridley and Cranmer – hence her nickname 'Bloody Mary'. She married a Catholic (Philip II of Spain) and subsequently joined Spain in a disastrous war against France. She lost Calais, which was England's last French possession.

Elizabeth I (1558–1603)

Daughter of Henry VIII and Anne Boleyn. After narrowly surviving accusations of being a traitor to her sister Mary, she eventually not only gained the throne upon Mary's death, but also kept it for 44 years. She returned England to Protestantism, but in contrast to her sister she was moderate in actions and beliefs. By skilful political manipulation she kept a strong hold on the reins of government and kept her kingdom intact. She kept everyone guessing about whom she would marry and then married no one. She was educated as well as clever, and was fluent in several languages. She had a keen eye for talent and was served by outstanding advisers.

The influence of Tudor monarchs upon the shape of the period was enormous, and their characters and actions need to be understood.

Why you need to know these facts

● Choose a Tudor monarch (different groups could be allocated a monarch each), and write an obituary for him or her. Include a portrait if you can. Use the Internet to find more information.
● In groups or as a class, make up a mnemonic or rhyme that will help you to remember the names and order of the Tudor monarchs.
● Write a script for a radio interview of a monarch from the Tudor period. Imagine that you are Jeremy Paxman or John Humphries – what would you like to ask the monarch, and how would they answer? You could act this out for a class assembly.

Teaching ideas

The wives of Henry VIII

Subject facts

Even by modern Hollywood standards, having six wives is an achievement of some note. Fortunately, the methods by which Henry disposed of one wife before moving on to the next is not something that happens today; and was shocking and callous even then.

Catherine of Aragon
She was the wife of Henry's dead brother Arthur. She gave birth to a daughter, the future Mary I, but in the absence of a male heir Henry divorced her without the Pope's consent, and broke the English Church away from Rome.

Anne Boleyn
Passionate love, while he was still married to Catherine, turned to passionate hate after the birth of Elizabeth (the future queen). Anne was accused of adultery and beheaded.

Jane Seymour
Bore Henry the son he craved, but died 12 days later.

Anne of Cleves
Anne turned out to be less of a beauty than Henry had been led to believe. He married her under protest to secure an alliance with German Protestants to balance the military threat from France and Spain. But when France and Spain, themselves at loggerheads, no longer posed the same degree of threat, the alliance and the marriage lost their purpose. Soon Henry had the marriage dissolved on grounds of non-consummation and Anne was pensioned off.

In their own words

> *I liked her before not well, now I like her much worse.*
> Henry VIII on Anne of Cleves

Catherine Howard
Catherine was much younger than Henry, and was a pawn in the hands of her ambitious uncles. Henry found out about her adultery and she was tried and beheaded.

Catherine Parr
An intelligent woman already twice widowed when Henry married her. Catherine's interest in radical Protestantism was nearly her undoing. When she agreed to yield to her husband in religious matters, investigations of her actions stopped on the king's orders. She nursed and outlived him.

The treatment of Henry's wives is significant in that it reveals the ruthlessness with which the passionate Henry could act. His actions affected the future of the Church and the succession.

For nine days in 1553, England was ruled by a young girl, Lady Jane Grey. She was proclaimed queen by a faction, led by the Duke of Northumberland, in an attempt to prevent the Catholic Mary Tudor from ascending the throne. The coup collapsed because Northumberland was widely detested. Jane Grey was beheaded. She was only 17.

Tradition (not evidence) has it that the Crown of England was found under a gorse bush after the battle of Bosworth and then placed on Henry Tudor's head.

● Make a chart that will help the children to learn and remember the names of the wives of Henry VIII and what happened to them.
● Learn how to dance a period dance that would have been popular at court. A Spanish Pavane is fairly straightforward.

Henry VIII and the break with Rome

Religious pressure for change already existed, and in many parts of Europe a Protestant reformation was taking place. Henry's need for money and a wife who would give him a male heir merely provided the occasion for the split from the Roman Church.

Henry wanted to divorce Catherine of Aragon and marry Anne Boleyn. He ordered his chief adviser in such matters, Cardinal Wolsey, to arrange his divorce by asking the Pope to agree. Wolsey failed and was sacked. Henry then cleared the way for his new wife by ignoring the Pope's view and divorcing Catherine. He cut all legal and financial ties with Rome and made himself head of the Church in England in an Act of Supremacy (1534).

Sir Thomas More (1478–1535) was one of the casualties of Henry's action. More was a scholar and a statesman – a Renaissance humanist. He rose to be Lord Chancellor but opposed the king's divorce and remarriage. When he opposed the Act of Supremacy he was beheaded.

Henry sent his Vicar General, Thomas Cromwell, to organize an audit of monastic life: he had his eyes on the extensive wealth of the monasteries. Many clerics still acknowledged the Pope as their leader and some lived like rich country gentlemen. Although monastic ideals were not always observed, Cromwell's reports were probably biased to satisfy the king's wishes. Henry was given, in Cromwell's reports, the ammunition to dissolve the monasteries and confiscate their wealth, which he did. Many beautiful buildings were destroyed when the monasteries were dissolved in 1536 – church plate was melted down for cash and the nuns and monks turned out onto the streets. It was not an unpopular measure at the time.

After Henry VIII died, the nature of religion in England continued to change. But for the Catholic interlude under Mary Tudor, England became more clearly Protestant in Tudor times. The Mass was renamed Holy Communion, many local Saint's days were abolished, and traditions like Plough Monday and Maypoles were stopped. A Book of Common Prayer was introduced for the first time in 1549.

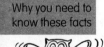

Why you need to know these facts

The Church of England resulted from the split with the Roman Catholic Church. This affected the way England has been governed since, the nature of the Church in England, and the subsequent course of this nation's history.

Teaching ideas

● Investigate the difference between Catholic and Protestant. Visit local churches or invite local incumbents to talk to the class.
● Listen to some Tudor music such as 'Greensleeves', written by Henry VIII for Anne Boleyn.
● Use the Internet to investigate monastic sites in Britain that were destroyed at the dissolution of the monasteries. Prepare brief 'tourist's guides' to some of the destinations, such as Fountains Abbey.

Henry VIII and the *Mary Rose*

In 1545 Francis I of France sent a fleet to attack England. With 235 ships and 30 000 men, it was larger than the Armada. It sailed round the Isle of Wight to attack Portsmouth and was met by an English fleet of 60 ships led by the *Great Harry* and the *Mary Rose*. Henry watched the battle from Southsea Castle. For reasons that are still not clear, the *Mary Rose* floundered. Water entered through her gunports and she sank so quickly that most of the crew drowned. Only about a dozen of the 700 crew survived. The French boasted that they had sunk the ship, but bad seamanship seems to be the most likely cause.

Subject facts

Tudor sea power began with Henry VIII, and he laid the foundations for English maritime exploits in the reign of Elizabeth I. He created an effective navy, which could compete with the maritime supremacy of Spain. Portsmouth dockyard was built, 80 ships were added to the navy and the navy and army were separated for the first time.

Why you need to know these facts

In 1982 the *Mary Rose* was raised from the sea bed. It provided an enormous amount of evidence about the crew and life on board a Tudor ship. Among the finds were 168 yew bows and 3000 arrows, each 79cm long, games, musical instruments, a surgeon's chest, tableware, sewing kits and clothes.

Amazing facts

● Investigate the mystery of the sinking of the *Mary Rose*. Is it a case of whodunnit? or whatdunnit?

Teaching ideas

Elizabeth I

Elizabeth remains one of the most remarkable British monarchs, and one of the most important in the Tudor dynasty. Elizabeth's skill at maintaining the integrity of her kingdom is legendary and she needed all her considerable intelligence to survive in the climate of intrigue that was the Tudor Court.

Subject facts

Mary Queen of Scots

One of Elizabeth's first problems was to deal with the threats to her throne that came from her cousin, Mary Stuart – Mary Queen of Scots. Mary, whose mother was French, spent 13 years in France. She was married briefly to the elderly French king, but he died after two years, and she was forced to return to Scotland. As a devout Catholic she did not last long when faced with a Protestant hierarchy there, especially the extremist Protestant reformer and misogynist John Knox. He wrote a book *The first Blast of the Trumpet against the Monstrous Regiment of Women.*

But Mary was an attractive woman and at first gained popularity with the people of Edinburgh. She married her cousin, the lusty womanizer Lord Darnley, thus strengthening her claim to the English throne (he was the grandson of Henry VIII's sister) but weakening her public and political image. Mary soon felt lonely and was neglected by her husband so she turned to David Riccio, her private secretary, for advice. Darnley became jealous and one night, Riccio was seized in the queen's presence and murdered on the stairs in Holyrood Palace. Darnley was there and Mary was forced to flee.

Intrigues continued; Mary fell in love with the Earl of Bothwell, then Darnley was mysteriously murdered. Bothwell was found not guilty of the crime after a farcical trial – but it was an intrigue too far. Mary married Bothwell and the Scots turned against her. She rapidly abdicated in favour of her infant son James and fled on horseback to England for safety.

Unfortunately, there she became the focus of Catholic plots. She was imprisoned and continued to plot against Elizabeth, who eventually, and reluctantly, had her executed for treason in 1587.

The marriage problem and Essex

The other problem which dogged Elizabeth was the constant attempt to marry her off. Marriage was, for a monarch, a matter of major political significance. First there was the need to secure the succession; then there was the matter of forging a political alliance through marriage (a very delicate matter); and thirdly there was always the question of a bad match handing power to an ambitious, unscrupulous or unsuitable man. Elizabeth solved the problem by keeping everyone guessing and ultimately not marrying at all.

There was, however, no shortage of suitors. Robert Devereux, the 2nd Earl of Essex, was one suspected lover. A clever, literate man, he soon became a favourite of Elizabeth but fell out of favour when his clandestine marriage was discovered. Nevertheless he rose to be a privy councillor and take the title Earl Marshall. He was strong-willed and hard to control. He had a great quarrel with Elizabeth when he turned his back on her, and she boxed his ears. The quarrel was never properly made up and after serving in Ireland he eventually ended up in prison. He formed a mad plot to remove Elizabeth's councillors and tried to start a rebellion in London. As a consequence he was beheaded in 1601.

Why you need to know these facts

The behaviour of the ruling classes, Tudor Court intrigues, and the love affairs of Tudor monarchs were of great significance in this period. The marriages of monarchs were not personal events, but political ones that could resolve conflicts or even cause wars.

Amazing facts

On one of her summer progresses, Queen Elizabeth stayed with Lord North for three days. Together with her entourage she consumed 1200 chickens, 67 sheep, 34 pigs, 33 geese and 2500 eggs.

Teaching ideas

● Examine Tudor costume through pictures. Make a collage reproduction of a famous portrait. Try to match the colours and stick to natural fabrics.

Tudor seafarers and explorers

John and Sebastian Cabot

Subject facts

John Cabot (1425–1500) and his son Sebastian (1474–1557) lived in Venice before making Bristol their home in about 1490. Enjoying the patronage of Henry VII, John sailed with his three sons from Bristol in 1497 in two ships. They looked for a north-west passage to the riches of the east; instead they found land not seen by Europeans since Viking times –

Nova Scotia and Cape Breton Island. Sebastian was a cartographer and worked for both the Spanish and Henry VIII. He was made inspector of the navy by Edward VI and in 1499 claimed credit for exploring the north-west passage, credit that should have been his father's.

John Hawkins (1532–1595)

John Hawkins was one of those swashbuckling adventurers who cut their teeth harrying Spanish treasure ships in the West Indies. But he was later appointed treasurer of Elizabeth's navy and helped to make it into the formidable force that was to defeat the Spanish Armada. His other major claim to fame is that he was one of the first Englishmen to run the trading route that led from Africa to Central America, carrying slaves. This brought him into direct conflict with the Spanish, which encouraged him into further piratical activity.

Francis Drake (c1540–1596)

Drake was one of the most successful privateers and a constant thorn in the side of the Spanish. In 1572, for example, with two ships and 73 men, he attacked a Spanish fleet near Nombre de Dios and captured so much treasure that he could not carry it all away. To the Spanish he was a pirate; to the English a hero at a time when England was contesting supremacy of the seas with the Spanish.

Under the sponsorship of Elizabeth I, Drake became the first Englishman to circumnavigate the globe (1577–1580). With five ships he set out to explore the Strait of Magellan, returning to England via the Cape of Good Hope. Only one ship, the *Golden Hind*, made it back to England and his search for a north-west passage also failed. But he sailed around Cape Horn, attacked Spanish ships on the Peruvian coast, and renamed California 'New Albion'. He crossed the Pacific Ocean and traded for spices in the Far East before returning to Plymouth.

Drake was involved in other state-sponsored adventures mainly aimed at acquiring treasure and weakening the fleets of Spain and Portugal. In 1587 Drake destroyed between two and three dozen Spanish ships in Cadiz where they were preparing for an invasion of England. This delayed the Armada for a year.

The Spanish Armada 1588

Drake (*Revenge*), Hawkins (*Victory*), Howard (*Ark Royal*) and Frobisher (*Triumph*) were part of a talented and experienced roll call of captains whose expertise and bravery helped to defeat the Spanish attempt to invade England in 1588. Spain was tired of the English interference with her treasure ships sailing from the New World and recognized that England was challenging Spanish supremacy at sea. But the hostility between the two countries ran deeper; Spain was Catholic, England was Protestant, and Philip of Spain had been Queen Mary's husband. For him it was a religious campaign to put a Catholic monarch back on the English throne. Elizabeth had been declared a usurper and a heretic and excommunicated by the Pope in 1570, so the Pope gave his blessing to Philip's crusade.

It was an ambitious move on the part of Philip of Spain. The Armada was commanded by the Duke Medina Sidonia (who was not a sailor and ill-suited to this command) and consisted of 130 ships manned by 8000 seamen. Also on board was the Army of Flanders (about 20 000 soldiers). Sidonia had orders to sail across the Channel and land near Margate before thrusting northwards towards London.

The Armada sailed up the Channel but the English fleet, under the command of Lord Howard of Effingham, harassed them. The English fleet was forced by the direction of the wind to wait until they were behind the Armada before setting sail, so they appeared to the west of the Spanish and snapped at their heels without inflicting much harm. Both sides expressed admiration for the seamanship of the other: the Spanish holding firm to a difficult crescent formation up the Channel; the English nipping around their flanks carefully avoiding getting surrounded by the larger Spanish vessels. Many suitable landing places were passed, because Medina Sidonia kept to his orders to go for the Margate area. The English, not knowing this, feared a landing on the Isle of Wight and continued to harass until the fleet anchored off Calais. Both fleets were by now running low on ammunition.

English fire ships were sent in at night, which caused the Spanish to panic and slip their moorings. Although the Spanish intended to return at daybreak, tides swept the Armada northwards. Spanish ships, now out of formation, became isolated and were attacked, and bad weather finally forced them to head for home round the north of Scotland. Many of the ships were wrecked; only 53 returned to Spain.

In spite of this disaster, other Armadas were planned, and in 1595 the Spanish again attacked, this time destroying Penzance, but other attempts were driven back by storms. In the early Stuart period (1604), peace was signed between England and Spain and there were no more Armadas.

Walter Ralegh and exploration

Walter (later Sir Walter) Ralegh is a Tudor figure worthy of study because he is representative of the explorers and seafarers that were responsible for extending knowledge of the New World and for increasing England's wealth and influence in Europe.

He was almost the model hero: six feet tall with thick black hair, educated (at Oxford), adventurous and brave. He could also be headstrong and was once thrown into prison for causing an affray in Westminster. Such a striking character was, perhaps, bound to be noticed at Court, where he rapidly became one of Queen Elizabeth's favourites. One story of how Ralegh came to the Queen's attention describes how Elizabeth was about to step out of her coach into a pool of water when the young Ralegh stepped forward and placed his cloak over the puddle. There is no historical proof that this actually happened, although the action would have been consistent with his gallant character.

Ralegh was responsible for making smoking fashionable at Court, but he was not responsible for bringing tobacco back to England in the first place – Ralegh received his tobacco from Drake.

'Piratical' is a good word to describe Ralegh's early career as an explorer. He sailed from the coast of Devon seeking not new lands, but Spanish treasure ships to plunder. After rising to an important position at Court, he was made Vice-Admiral of the Western Counties and given the title Sir Walter Ralegh. He spent a great deal of his own money trying to build a colony in Virginia but without much success, although he brought back the potato plant. Potatoes were first planted at one of Ralegh's homes in Ireland.

It is as a seafarer that Ralegh lays most of his claim to fame. He fought against the Spanish at Cadiz (and was wounded); he searched for gold in South America, and captured and plundered Spanish treasure ships. He had another spell in prison for angering the queen by having an affair with one of her maids and finally, when the queen died, his enemies conspired to get him confined to the Bloody Tower as a traitor. He spent years as a prisoner carrying out experiments, making medicines and writing a history of the world. But Queen Elizabeth had been his main protector, and when he failed to find gold in South America after being released from prison, he was doomed. Partly to appease the Spanish, who desired to see the end of Ralegh, he was beheaded in 1618, aged 66.

This was the time when Europeans explored huge areas of the world, in effect for the first time. The Tudors may have been searching for routes to the spices of the Orient or for new land or gold, but in doing so they colonized continents, opened trade routes, and introduced new foods and goods to Europe. Their legacy shaped today's world.

Why you need to know these facts

● Many of the risky journeys of exploration by sea were made seeking a route to the east and valuable spices. Today spices are commonplace, but in Tudor times men risked everything to trade in cargoes such as nutmeg, cinnamon, cloves, mace, pepper and ginger.

Amazing facts

● A sailor's diet was so poor that scurvy (lack of Vitamin C) killed many on long journeys – an estimated 10 000 died during Elizabeth's reign from this cause. Live animals were taken on board for lengthy sea voyages if possible and dried fish, rice, ship's biscuits, lentils, cheese, chickpeas and salted meat. Wine was preferred to water, which soon turned green on board and became undrinkable.

Drake played bowls while the Armada approached.
In fact the English did have to wait for the Armada to pass to windward before they could sail, and perhaps Drake did play bowls before he sailed. But the only evidence is a comment, years after the event, made by a Spanish writer that 'the English were at bowls upon the Hoe at Plymouth'.

Common misconceptions

The common spelling of Ralegh is Raleigh.
Ralegh was never spelled *Raleigh* in his lifetime, although today you will see both spellings. Modern historians, as opposed to school textbook writers, favour Ralegh as that was the way he himself spelled his name.

● Investigate which foods were brought to the Tudor table from newly discovered lands.
● Find out about life on board a Tudor ship. How did the sailors tell the time? What kinds of food did they eat? How did they navigate?
● On an outline map of the world, mark the places that were visited by famous Tudor sailors. You may be able to plot some of their voyages.
● Have a celebration of a old Tudor tradition which has long since been abolished, such as Maypole dancing.

Teaching ideas

Elizabethan theatre

Actors and the theatre were, for a long time, regarded as wicked. Puritans once banned plays, and women were not allowed on the stage. Instead, boys played female parts. But in later Tudor times, the world of the travelling player, scraping a living on the edge of legality by performing in the open air or inn yards, changed forever. Queen Elizabeth enjoyed plays, so performing and writing them gradually became more respectable. In 1577, James Burbage at Shoreditch erected the first purpose-built playhouse, called *The Theatre*. His son Richard built *The Globe* in 1599.

William Shakespeare (1564–1616)

Shakespeare was born on St George's day (23rd April) in the same year as Christopher Marlowe. He was the son of a glover from Stratford upon Avon, and his mother, Mary Arden, was a farmer's daughter. He was given a decent education in Stratford and, having married Anne Hathaway, another farmer's daughter, he made his home in London. In the early 1590s he was performing on the stage with Richard Burbage. He formed a relationship with the Burbages and wrote many plays for them. Gradually he began to acquire fame and fortune and purchased a house and land in Stratford in preparation for retirement. He had three daughters, Susanna and twins Hamnet and Judith.

As well as many plays, he wrote over 150 sonnets and narrative poems. Shakespeare had an unequalled genius that flowered at a time when the performance of plays was becoming respectable.

The theatre as we know it began in the late 16th century. This is the era of Shakespeare, arguably the greatest poet and playwright the world has ever known.

● The stealing of plots was rife in Shakespeare's time and still goes on. The musical *West Side Story* is a reworking of Shakespeare's *Romeo and Juliet*.

● Write a newspaper report of a visit to the Tudor theatre.
Remember the cutpurses as well as the play.

Resources

You will not have to look far for places to visit in England
and you are likely to have a worthwhile museum or historic
site in your county. Most of the places worth visiting are also
worth contacting for resources and teachers' packs.

Websites
Tudor dance music: www.gOnen.demon.co.uk/dance.htm
English Heritage: www.eng-h.gov.uk/
Tudor dynasty: www.royal.gov.uk/history
Shakespeare: www.stratford.co.uk/birthplace/new.html

Books
The Tudors are a popular subject for writers and there are
many textbooks and information books aimed at junior
children. The following are particularly useful for teachers:
Food and Cooking in 16th Century Britain by Peter Brears
(English Heritage).
Tudor Chester Teacher's Resource Pack, Chester Education,
Grosvenor Museum, 27 Grosvenor Street, Chester CH1 2DD.
Voyages and Discoveries by Richard Hakluyt (pub. 1598/
1600); edited by J Beeching (Penguin Classics) – contains
Drake's circumnavigation and the Armada account.
Learning from Country Houses by Christopher Culpin (The
National Trust) – a resource book for teachers.
A Teacher's Guide to Using Portraits by Susan Morris
(English Heritage) – full of practical suggestions.
Tudor Times by Jo Lawrie and Paul Noble (Collins).

Books for children
Daily life in a Tudor House by Laura Wilson (Hamlyn).
Then and There series (8 titles on the Elizabethan World) by
Marjorie Reeves (Longman).
Look Inside A Tudor Warship by Brian Moses (Wayland).
Queen Elizabeth I by Peggy Burns (Wayland).
On the Trail of the Tudors in Britain by Richard Wood
(Franklin Watts).

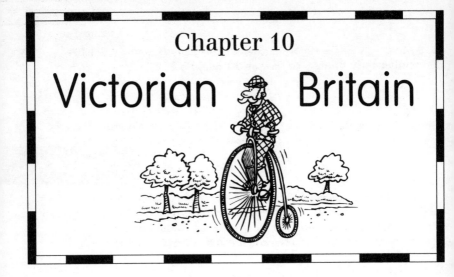

Chapter 10
Victorian Britain

During the reign of Queen Victoria, Britain established a vast Empire and became the most powerful and wealthy nation in the world. The Victorian legacy remains very conspicuous in Britain today – most hospitals, schools and a large part of the housing stock are Victorian, and people still refer to *Victorian values*. Although the Empire has long since disintegrated it is responsible for making Britain the multi-ethnic country that it is today.

Introducing the Victorians

Timeline

1837	*Queen Victoria ascends the throne aged 18 years.*
	Fox Talbot invents photography.
1840	*Victoria marries Prince Albert.*
	Houses of Parliament and Nelson's Column erected.
	Transport of criminals to New South Wales ends.
	Penny Post introduced.
1842	*The Mines Act stops children under 10 working in the mines.*
	Income Tax introduced.
1844	*Factory Act limits children's working hours in factories to six and a half hours a day.*
1851	*Great Exhibition in Hyde Park (Crystal Palace).*

Crimean War.	1854–56
Prince Albert dies of typhoid.	1861
The Queen's Silver Jubilee (25 years).	1862
First cricket tour of Australia.	
Education Act sets up Board Schools to provide schools in every area.	
Alexander Graham Bell invents the telephone.	
Education becomes compulsory.	1880
Queen Victoria's Golden Jubilee (50 years).	1887
First Sherlock Holmes novel written by Arthur Conan-Doyle.	
First Ediswan (Edison and Swan) electric lightbulb.	
Baden-Powell founds the Boy Scouts.	
First underground electric railway opens in London.	1900
Queen Victoria dies aged 81 years.	1901

How do we know about the Victorians?

Evidence about the Victorians is overwhelming in quantity. They created much of the urban landscape of Britain, and if we look around it is not long before we see a Victorian house, shop, park or statue. Street names are often Victorian, there may even be a Victorian postbox on a nearby corner.

Documentary evidence of every kind also abounds, but in particular we have regular and systematic government records (the census, for example) kept by law for the first time. We also have official maps (another first) and photographs. The Victorians invented photography and they played with it like a new toy. Photographs bring a new dimension to our knowledge of the past and the Victorian period is the first for which such evidence is available.

Victorian society

Rich and poor

Subject facts

Many factory owners in the 19th century became very wealthy and the large houses of these newly rich families can still be seen around Britain's industrial towns today. One of the strange facts about Victorian Britain is that within such a wealthy nation abject poverty could still exist. It worried people at the time: the rich got richer, the nation got richer, hospitals, schools, parks and public buildings were erected on a grand scale, yet the Victorians constantly struggled with the problem of the poor. It was the stuff of parliamentary debate, legislation and literature.

The problem, which threatened to overwhelm the Victorians, was probably the result of their success. The population of Britain grew at an astonishing rate: in 30 years the population of London grew from 4 million to 6.5 million (1871–1901). Nevertheless, better food, housing and clothing caused the high Victorian mortality rates to start to decline and the lot of the poor generally improved. Birth rates were high and houses were needed quickly so they tended to be built speedily and without proper care. Perhaps the real surprise is that the Victorians coped with the problem as well as they did. During the Victorian period, the quality of housing did gradually improve for the majority of people, but for the poorest 20 per cent it was probably as bad at the beginning of the 20th century as it had been at the beginning of Victoria's reign.

During the latter part of the century there was a growth in the number of charities set up to deal with the problems of poverty, such as The Poor Children's Boot Fund, The Country Holiday Society, and the School's Cheap Dinner Society. There were also state efforts to improve living conditions; indeed the Victorians became very public health conscious. Local Authorities established by the Victorians began to regulate shops and organize street cleaning. Water supplies and sewage disposal became a priority.

Workhouses

From early in the period (1834) workhouses had been set up to cater for the destitute – but these were dire places. In 1840 there was a public outcry when it was discovered that the inmates of Andover Workhouse were so hungry that they were gnawing bones they had been given to crush into fertilizer.

The middle classes

Middle-class houses were large and so were most families. This meant that there was plenty of employment for servants; butlers, cooks, gardeners and maids were employed to do the menial tasks of the house: cleaning the grates, laying tables, emptying slop buckets and so on. Some servants lived in, and were often accommodated 'below stairs' in fairly cramped conditions.

Running a large home was far more labour-intensive than it is today, but technological advances began to decrease the drudgery in the last decades of the century (flushing lavatories, vacuum cleaners, electric ovens and kettles, for example). Although uniforms, board and lodgings were provided for servants, their lives were closely controlled (advertisements required 'no followers', which meant no boyfriends) and wages were very low. An important servant such as a cook might earn £25 a year but a scullery maid might earn as little as £9 a year and have little time off for seeing her family.

Holidays and entertainment

Towards the end of the century people had more money and more time to enjoy themselves. Watching and taking part in sport became a national pastime and most well-known British sporting events like the FA Cup Final date from this period, as do many national sporting organizations. The Wimbledon Tennis Championships began in 1874 and the Football Association started to organize the professional game in 1848. Cycling became incredibly popular; the Cyclists Touring Club was founded in 1878 and there were over 2000 local cycling clubs by 1901.

Travel was relatively easy and cheap. People were able to get out into the countryside under their own steam or by railway. The Victorians virtually invented the idea of 'the seaside', and special railway excursion trains sped them to where they could stroll along the promenade or walk on a pier constructed specially for that purpose. Seaside places close to big industrial centres were extremely popular and could become dominated by workers from particular cities when their factories closed for the local holidays (places such as Blackpool, Bridlington, Skegness and Southend). Thomas Cook started his travel firm in 1841 and made a big profit running excursion trains to the Great Exhibition.

Going abroad on a cultural tour became popular with the wealthy – often it was seen as part of the education of a young person. Queen Victoria set an example by favouring holidays abroad, and the wealthy British helped contribute to the creation of the holiday resorts of northern France and the Riviera. For many in the Civil Service and the military, of course, the Empire gave them the opportunity to see the world.

But there was plenty of pleasure to be had at home. Working-class theatres, called 'music halls', were very popular for a night out and audiences flocked to see stars such as Lillie Langtry and Marie Lloyd. Public houses also grew in popularity with the working classes causing an increase in the problem of alcoholism. Organizations such as the Salvation Army and the Temperance Movement fought hard to rescue people from such excesses.

Why you need to know these facts

Understanding the past is about understanding people and the way they lived. Even though the Victorian age was a period of astonishing invention and technological change, it is the impact that these advances had on the lives of individuals that is important.

Amazing facts

● In the 1860s the average Victorian family had five or six children.

Teaching ideas

● The children could create a Victorian portrait gallery of leading figures from the period. They could draw information and pictures from the Internet or simply create 'pen' portraits. Groups of children could play a game of 'Who's who?', matching descriptions with characters from the portrait gallery.
● Set up a classroom museum of Victorian artefacts and pictures (check the school contents insurance first). Your local museum service may loan out items and children could be encouraged to bring things to school (coins, stamps, samplers, irons, washing dollies and so on).

Queen Victoria and her family

Subject facts

Although Queen Victoria was not a powerful ruler in the old sense, she lived for a long time and left her mark, not only on the period, but also on generations after her. She gave her name to an age.

The Queen
Victoria became queen as a girl of 18 and reigned for longer than any other British monarch, before or since. Her rule lasted 63 years. She was born in Kensington Palace in 1819 to the fourth son of George III. She married her cousin, Prince Albert of Saxe-Coburg in 1840. Prince Albert died at the early age of 42, but she bore him nine children – five boys and four girls. At her Diamond Jubilee in 1897 she had 29 grandchildren.

Most of Victoria's children married into other royal families in Europe. Her eldest son, Edward, married Alexandra, daughter of Christian IX of Denmark and later became Edward VII. Victoria was a lively child with a talent for drawing and painting. She was not unintelligent, and when she was queen she learned Hindustani so that she could talk with her favourite Indian servants. She also liked to keep a diary, which has revealed many details about her life and attitudes, although her daughter Beatrice destroyed some of this valuable evidence after her mother's death.

Victoria was besotted with Albert and their marriage was a very happy one. After Albert's death in 1861, Victoria went into a prolonged period of mourning from which she never fully recovered. She became known as the *Widow of Windsor* and refused to be seen in public – even to open Parliament – and this made her very unpopular. But she lived long and her feelings changed. In 1876 she was given the title *Empress of India*.

Because of her family ties to many of the rulers in Europe, she was also called the *Grandmother of Europe*. Victoria, the Princess Royal, married Friedrich III the German Emperor, and this provided a strong Anglo-German link that proved embarrassing when the First World War started.

In their own words

> *We are not interested in the possibilities of defeat; they do not exist.*
> Queen Victoria visiting troops after a British reversal in battle

Prince Albert and the Great Exhibition of 1851

Albert was never popular in his lifetime, partly because he was foreign, and also because he attempted to promote liberal and progressive movements in the country. But, as the Prince Consort, he did have influence, and the Queen doted on him. The Great Exhibition was one of Albert's successes. With his support and the organizational skill of Henry Cole, the Exhibition preparations forged ahead in the face of initial public apathy and some outright opposition. But the idea gained momentum; public subscriptions to fund the project were sought, and the Queen herself donated £1000.

The Exhibition was intended to be about industrial progress, trade and the superiority of British design. The themes were Progress, Work, Religion and Peace. There

were over 100 000 exhibits and price labels were strictly
forbidden. It was an amazing success – even the public
toilets made a profit. People came on day excursions using
the new and extensive railway network, some using trains
for the first time. On the busiest day, 93 224 visitors entered
the building.

The building itself was a wonder. The design, by Joseph
Paxton, was chosen as the result of a competition that
produced 233 entries. The building was erected in Hyde
Park originally and was made of cast iron and glass, hence
the name *Crystal Palace*. It took six months to complete.
The building did not remain there long and was moved to
Sydenham when the exhibition closed. It was over three
times the length of St Paul's Cathedral and contained
293 655 panes of glass.

The profit from the Exhibition, some £186 000, was used
to purchase the South Kensington sites upon which many
of London's leading public buildings were erected
(including, for example, the Victoria and Albert Museum
and the Albert Hall).

Why you need to know these facts

It is necessary to understand that Britain's power and
influence in the Victorian era was founded on its great
industrial muscle and wealth. The Great Exhibition was a
symbol and celebration of this wealth, and also an
expression of the pride the Victorians took in their
achievements. It also marked a significant moment in the
development of cheap travel for the masses, and of the
beginning of excursion travel.

Amazing facts

● Queen Victoria looms large historically but was actually
quite small. She was just 1.5 metres (5 feet) tall.
● Paxton's great building eventually gave its name to a
south London suburb and to a leading football team.
● Visitors to the Crystal Palace consumed 2 million buns
and 1 million bottles of lemonade.

Common misconceptions

Queen Victoria was not amused.
She was a lively child and enjoyed much of her life, even
after the death of Albert. She was the most widely travelled
monarch ever at the time and spent much of her time on
holiday in France and Scotland. She did, however, mourn
her beloved Albert for an inordinate length of time and held
rather rigid views.

● By 1900 the British Empire had grown enormously. Map its extent using coloured pencils (traditionally using red for the Empire). What has happened to these countries now?
● Choose a Victorian invention (the telephone, the electric light, trams, and so on), and tell its story. Say what good things have resulted from its invention and what bad things.
● If you were planning a Great Exhibition today on the same themes as in 1851, what would you include in it?

Teaching ideas

The railway age

George Stephenson

James Watt invented the first steam-powered engine in 1788, and Richard Trevithick invented the first locomotive based on Watt's design in 1804. But the real beginning of the railway dates from 1825, when George Stephenson (1781–1848) built a railway to carry coal from Stockton to Darlington. The early railways carried heavy goods and were relatively slow. Robert Stephenson (1803–1859), son of George, entered a competition (Rainhill, 1829) to build an engine to run from Liverpool to Manchester. His *Rocket* won it with a top speed of around 40km/h (29mph).

Subject facts

Railway expansion

Within a few years, this line was joined to Birmingham and then to London (1839). A period of intense building began when railways were built everywhere, sometimes even where they were not economically viable. Investors could not wait to part with their money to aid railway building and the 1840s became a time of 'railway mania'. Gangs of unruly navvies descended on the countryside causing mayhem and even terror in some areas; cuttings were dug (by hand), tunnels excavated, and bridges built. Railway building was a highly visible activity.

By 1850 Britain had over 8000 kilometres (5000 miles) of track, which grew to over 28 000 kilometres (18 000 miles) by the end of the century. This was the end of the stagecoach era and use of canals began to decline, although they continued to be used for heavy goods such as coal.

Isambard Kingdom Brunel

During the period of railway mania, the world's first covered station was built at Temple Meads in Bristol in

1840. This was the brainchild of the astonishingly gifted Victorian engineer, Isambard Kingdom Brunel (1806–1859). He was the son of an English engineer who was French-born, but settled in England in the late 18th century. He liked to be involved in every detail of his designs and was a formidable taskmaster. He would turn his hand to most things, designing trackside buildings for the Great Western Railway, the Clifton Suspension Bridge in Bristol, and transatlantic steamships. His ship *The Great Eastern*, built in 1858, remained the world's largest until 1899.

His great railway achievement was the line from London to Bristol, built on a broad gauge. He constructed the Box Tunnel and Paddington Station, and created the railway town of Swindon virtually on a whim. (The small nearby settlement of Swindon was known as 'Old Town' to distinguish it from Brunel's railway village near the canal. The name has stuck to this day.)

Why you need to know these facts

The economic impact of the railways on Britain was enormous. The railways enabled industries to expand (especially coal and steel) and goods to become cheaper. This greatly enhanced the wealth of the nation and employment opportunities. There was demand generated, at home and abroad, for the railway-engineering skills that Britain possessed. Almost no aspect of life was untouched; the ports expanded to cope with increased trade, and the speedy distribution of goods meant that mass production and the standardization of products increased. People could travel easily to work and this led to suburban expansion. They could also travel easily to the seaside or the Great Exhibition.

With the coming of the railways communication generally improved. Newspapers travelled swiftly, delivery of mail was speeded up and the equipment of war could be transported more readily. By rail, the journey from Liverpool to London took six and a half hours; previously it had taken 24 hours by stagecoach.

Amazing facts

● When the Liverpool–Manchester railway opened on 15th September 1830, the Liverpool Member of Parliament, William Huskisson, was struck by Stephenson's *Rocket* and fatally injured, thus becoming the first railway fatality. Stephenson himself drove the train carrying the dying Huskisson to hospital in Manchester at the then unprecedented speed of 50km/h (36mph).

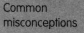
One single person invented the railway.
Like many great inventions railways were the culmination of discoveries, inventions and bright ideas involving a number of people. Watt, Trevithick and the Stephensons (George and Robert) should each take some credit, as should whoever first thought of using parallel tracks to aid the movement of heavy loads (we don't know who). The invention continues to be refined to this day.

Common misconceptions

● What would it be like to travel in a train pulled by Stephenson's *Rocket*? Investigate first, then write a newspaper report of an imaginary journey.
● Where have all the railways gone? Examine old Ordnance Survey maps (copies are available in any reference library) to draw the routes of Victorian lines near you that have disappeared. Find out all you can about them.

Teaching ideas

Factories and industrial towns

The Industrial Revolution

Subject facts

With the invention of machines powered by steam or water, the way in which people worked and lived changed completely. This was the Industrial Revolution and it began in Britain in the late 18th century. By the time Queen Victoria came to the throne new inventions had created a demand for more power and more factories. Although the first factories were in the country close to sources of power (they were often called mills), factories needed workers so towns expanded to meet the demand for labour. When there was little work on the land people were forced to seek work in the growing industrial towns. Cotton, imported from America and the British colonies, provided the raw material for textile manufacture, which became Britain's foremost industry. But despite the movement of labour towards the cities, farming and the rural life remained a major part of Britain's make-up.

Working in a factory
Conditions in the new factories were far from healthy. Everything was geared to the rhythm of the machines to maximize production and generally little thought was given to safe or healthy working conditions. Small children as

young as seven were commonly employed to work in textile mills where their size allowed them to crawl amongst the machines to fix broken threads and do other tasks. They could be forced to work for 16 hours a day, six days a week.

Some factory owners were caring and far-sighted, and made enormous efforts to look after their workers, sometimes building homes, schools, churches and hospitals just for them. Quakers, such as George and Richard Cadbury led the way by building the model village of Bournville in Birmingham to house their workers. But mostly factory workers were treated like parts of the machines on which they worked. Children were beaten for minor offences, and workers fined for anything that might slow down production such as whistling or opening a window. In the engine shop in the Great Western factory in Swindon, the toilets were made so foul that workers avoided using them.

Coal and mining

Factories using steam power generated an enormous demand for coal. Coal was plentiful but it had to be mined, which was a dangerous job. Until 1842, when Shaftesbury's law prohibited it, young children and women worked underground in the mines.

Why you need to know these facts

Factories are with us still today, but during the Victorian period there was a real boom in factory building. It was the factory, mass-producing goods often round the clock, that produced the wealth upon which Britain's power and prosperity was built.

Amazing facts

● The invention of spinning and weaving machines led to the establishment of huge factories. Swainson and Birley's factory near Preston was one of the biggest, measuring 144.5 metres long, 16.5 metres broad and seven stories high. It had 660 windows, and contained a remarkable 32 500 panes of glass.

● Sir Titus Salt (1803–1876) owned six factories, campaigned to give working men the vote, and funded the building of working men's clubs and chapels. In 1850 he decided to build a new model industrial village for his textile workers in Bradford. It was called Saltaire. Houses, shops and even a park were built between 1852 and 1872, and still exist today.

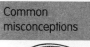

Farming declined during the Industrial Revolution.
In spite of the growth of factories, agriculture did not
decline. There was a boom in farming caused by the
demand a growing population made for food.

● Design an advertising campaign against child labour in a
factory or a coalmine.
● Many famous shops were founded in Victorian times.
Investigate and tell the story of one of them, either a local
one or one that is well known nationally, for example Boots
or John Lewis.
● Interrogate census returns for a particular year and
street. (These are sometimes available as a computer
printout or on floppy disk. Check with your county history
adviser.) Re-people a street, finding out as much as possible
about individuals who lived there. (You could make a visual
presentation along a corridor wall.) Find out all you can
about the work that people did.

Schools and childhood

Education pre-1870

Schools did exist when Queen Victoria came to the throne,
but they were mainly private grammar schools for the rich
and middle classes, and very expensive boarding and public
schools for the aristocracy. Girls from wealthy families
might be educated at home, but the poor had very little
chance of education. 'Dame schools', run in the homes of
local women, provided a very basic education for a small
fee, but there was an increasing need for an educated
workforce, as well as an educated electorate, and the
Victorians realized that this situation could not continue.

Charitable societies, set up by church groups, established
monitorial schools which attracted some government
grants. For example, the Church of England established one
school in rural Wiltshire in 1842 'for the poor of the Parish'.
As the government paid out more and more money, it
introduced payment by results (1862), with set tests in
reading, writing and arithmetic, to ensure that its money
was not wasted.

The 1870 Education Act

The year 1870 was a turning point. The 1870 Education Act established state schools wherever a church or charity school did not already exist. These were most often in the newly expanding towns and were called 'Board Schools', because the law provided for local authorities to set up 'Boards' to run them. At first education was neither free nor compulsory, but gradually this situation changed. Some local School Boards made attendance compulsory for children between the ages of 5 and 13 (for example, in London), but the Mundella Act of 1880 eventually made attendance obligatory for all children from 5 to 10. Secondary education as we know it did not arrive until the 20th century.

During the period of payment by results (from 1862), teachers concentrated on the 'three Rs' (and the fourth, Registration!) that ensured that the school was financed, so there was a great deal of learning by rote and strict discipline, coupled with attendance medals and rewards for those who came regularly. The abacus, the slate and the cane were key pieces of teaching equipment. Later the curriculum broadened to include geography, art and creative subjects. Religion was also important.

Childhood

Childhood as we know it is a modern invention. Babies of both sexes up to about the age of five were dressed and treated alike until recent times. After the age of seven they were treated like adults – two children of 7 and 11 were hanged as recently as 1708. In Victorian times these attitudes persisted. Child labour was common amongst the poor, where children were expected to contribute to the household as soon as possible. Middle-class children could live happy and secure lives, but we know from Victorian surveys and the writing of people like Charles Dickens that the lot of the poor could be execrable. Parliament had to bring in laws to limit working hours and to encourage education. But in the home, older children had to look after younger ones, do household tasks, clean boots, fetch water, carry coal, darn, sew and cook.

Small children were ideal for tasks such as chimney sweeping, and the law was slow in clamping down on such exploitation. Destitute and orphaned children were also a problem and there were many child beggars on the streets, as attested by the investigative journalist Henry Mayhew. Dr Thomas Barnardo set up the East End Mission in 1867 to care for homeless children. His National Incorporated

Association for the Reclamation of Destitute Waif Children became known as Dr Barnardo's Homes.

Education increased in importance as more and more people were given the vote. The Victorians realized that they must 'educate their masters'. Thus began the state education system that we have today, and to understand it you need to know how it evolved.

Why you need to know these facts

● Out of 17 614 elementary schools in 1880, only 3443 were Board Schools. The rest were voluntary schools run by the church or charities.
● By the end of the 19th century, illiteracy, as measured from Parish Registers, had almost been eliminated. The figures for both sexes were approximately the same, 97 per cent literate.

Amazing facts

Victorian education was harsh and narrow.
Indeed, it tended to be under the Revised Code (1862). But towards the end of the century, with the abolition of the Code, things began to change, and there is evidence of various enlightened individuals who used the locality as a teaching resource and realized the value of encouragement as well as punishment and of first-hand experience as well as rote learning.

Common misconceptions

● Compare 'then and now' using Victorian buildings, for example Victorian school/modern school; Victorian concert hall/modern concert hall. Identify and describe the main differences and similarities.
● Investigate evidence from a Victorian School Log Book. If you do not have one in school, your local record office should be able to help. Analyse entries for a year under different headings such as: discipline, buildings, holidays, the inspectors, and the curriculum. Compare with today.
● Create a Victorian Trail around your school/village/town. You could make a guide book or map using photographs.
● Practise some Victorian domestic tasks such as carpet beating, washing by hand, using a feather duster. Try cooking a Victorian dish (check a copy of *Mrs Beeton*).
● Have a Victorian school day. Research the topic first to make it as authentic as possible – see the Resources section

Teaching ideas

at the end of this chapter for further ideas on reference
sources.
● The Victorians built more churches than anyone since
the Normans and created the interior look of churches that
mostly survives to this day. Visit a suitable church and make
sketches of Victorian features. Make a visual guide to the
Victorian church.

The Crimean War

The War

The Crimean War (1854–56) was fought on the Crimean
peninsula in the Black Sea. Britain and France, as allies of
Turkey, fought (as they saw it) to restrain the expansion of
Russia. Fear of the 'Russian Bear' was a recurring theme of
19th century politics. Although the battles took place in the
Crimea, it was the more uneventful effect of the fleet
blockade of Russia in the Baltic that actually crippled the
Russian economy and precipitated the end of the conflict. In
the Crimea itself, the overriding impression, as far as the
British contribution was concerned, was one of
incompetence, bravery and defeat. In fact it was Russia that
was crippled, who accepted the Allies' terms, and took 50
years to recover from the effects of the war.

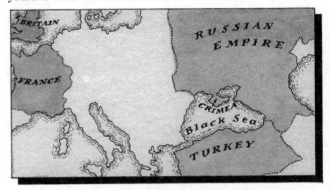

The origins of the war date back to a petty struggle
between France and Russia about who should control
certain Christian shrines in Palestine, but it was really
about defending the balance of power in Europe, power
struggles and the upholding of alliances.
The ghastly battles of Alma, Balaklava and Inkerman,
and the destruction of the British army in the winter of

1854–5 through neglect and stupidity was reported in *The Times* by William Russell. This had a great effect upon public opinion in Britain. For the first time they were able to appreciate the horrors and the mistakes of war. The government came under pressure to remedy matters.

The Russians held on to Sevastapol through the first winter, during which the French and British armies suffered enormously. Cutting supply routes by using the navy eventually brought about the fall of Sevastapol, and from then until peace was struck the exhausted armies did little more than watch each other across the Sea of Azov.

The charge of the Light Brigade took place about five kilometres (three miles) north of Balaklava and illustrates the blunder and bravado that typified the British conduct. Although it was a great disaster, Lord Tennyson, focused on the glory and made virtue out of failure.

In their own words

Half a league, half a league
Half a league and onward.
All in the Valley of Death
Rode the six hundred.
'Forward the Light Brigade!
Charge for the guns!' he said:
Into the Valley of Death
Rode the six hundred.
'The Charge of the Light Brigade', Alfred Lord Tennyson

Florence Nightingale

Florence Nightingale (1820–1910) was a stubborn, determined and independent woman who, despite opposition, trained as a nurse in Europe. After the Battle of Alma, she volunteered to go to the Crimea and organize the nursing of the wounded at Scutari. Using the support of influential friends, she was able to make the journey with 38 nurses. Soon she had 10 000 sick men under her care. She saw that the unsanitary conditions were the cause of the high mortality rate amongst the wounded, and set about remedying the causes.

Because of her romanticized image as 'the Lady with the Lamp', it is often forgotten how formidable her achievements were. She returned to England and set about reforming the training of nurses. Indeed, she spent the rest of her life tackling nursing issues, army sanitary reform, as well as public health in India. She became something of a public institution, living to the ripe old age of 90.

Why you need to know these facts

The Crimean War was the nearest the Victorians came to fighting a major war. It was incredibly expensive, and a drain upon the public purse; it revealed the inadequacies of military organization and training, and the class-ridden nature of the officer corps. It also started a revolution in both the reporting of war and in provision for the wounded and sick. Florence Nightingale was a critical figure in moving forward reforms in medical services that started in the Crimea but extended well beyond it.

Amazing facts

Florence Nightingale's book, *Notes on Nursing*, was so popular it was reprinted many times.

Common misconceptions

At the Charge of the Light Brigade, 600 soldiers rode into the Valley of Death.
Actually, it was nearer to 700 (*The Times* report at the time said 607).

Teaching ideas

● Research Florence Nightingale. Look for evidence to support what was said about her: interfering, boastful, given to tantrums, unselfish, calm, angelic, extraordinary.

The British Empire

Subject facts

For most of the duration of the Empire, the British were never quite sure whether having one was a good thing or not. At the end of the 18th century Britain lost the troublesome American colonies but gained, almost accidentally, vast areas of the sparsely inhabited globe – Canada, Australia and New Zealand. Gradually, through the reign of Queen Victoria, Britain extended the territories under its control in India, Africa and the Far East. The acquisition of territory was sometimes bloodless, sometimes bloody; exploration of Africa led to new land being annexed, and competition with other European powers gave impetus to empire building in the last decades of the century. Enthusiasm for the Empire waned after the expensive and disastrous Boer War in Africa, and the process of turning colonies into fully independent dominions was accelerated.

The Empire was built on trade. Britain imported raw materials such as cotton and rubber from colonies in the Empire and exported its manufactured goods, such as railway engines and tools, back to those same colonies. Britain created the world's most powerful navy to protect its trade routes and the Empire. Historians disagree as to whether the economic advantages of Empire outweighed its cost in the long term; at the time, some 19th-century politicians thought that the Empire was 'a millstone around Britain's neck' (Disraeli, 1852), others were enthusiastic imperialists.

Perhaps the two chief legacies of the Empire (there are numerous others, from Paisley design to bungalows!) are a multi-ethnic Britain and the use of the English language across the globe. British imperialists gave all sorts of ideas, buildings and institutions to the world, and the Empire gave similar in return, to such an extent that the culture of these islands was changed forever.

At the end of the 19th century the British had an empire which spanned the globe. It is too large to be ignored and too influential on the present to be forgotten.

Why you need to know these facts

Before she died, Queen Victoria ruled over nearly one quarter of the world's population and the British Empire had become the largest the world has ever known.

Teaching ideas

● Investigate the Commonwealth. On an outline map of the world compare the extent of the Commonwealth with the Empire at the end of the 19th century.
● Make a list of all the empires in history that you know about. Write down, in two columns, what you think were all the good things and all the bad things about them.

Resources

Except for a diminishing handful of people, the Victorian era is now beyond living memory. You may still be able to use elderly people who can recount information told to them by their parents and grandparents about life in the 19th century. But the wonderful thing about teaching the Victorian period is that evidence accessible to children is in plentiful supply. Many children will be being taught in a Victorian school, may live in a Victorian house, or may have walked to school through a Victorian park, past a Victorian postbox or near a Victorian town hall.

Documentary evidence is extensive. Consult your local archives, the reference library and look in the school itself. There are some excellent pamphlets that give concise details of these and other useful documents, or that state where to find them and their origins. Try *Short Guides to Records* – 48 titles in the series – available from the *Historical Association, 59a Kennington Park Road, London SE11 4JH* or online at www.history.org.uk

Extracts from Victorian books such as *Tom Brown's Schooldays* and *Lark Rise to Candleford* can be used selectively. Henry Mayhew's articles, originally published in the mid-19th century, are a powerful source of evidence if used selectively: *London Labour and the London Poor* Henry Mayhew (Penguin). For a perspective on the lives of women, see the evidence collected in *Ordinary Lives* by Carol Adams (Virago). Historical fiction can 'set the scene' , for example *Butty Boy* by Jill Paton-Walsh.

Chapter 11

Britain since 1930

A great deal has happened to Britain since 1930, and there are many people still alive who have lived through the changes. History is, in this case, still part of memory, and there has never been a period of history so comprehensively recorded by electronic and other means. The amount of evidence available is overwhelming. Every historical study is selective (you can never know everything about the past), but in the case of this period, it is particularly important to select and to remain focused on the topics you have chosen to study. Otherwise you will either become confused by the mass of detail, or wander into a study of contemporary affairs.

Most of the changes to the lives of people in Britain since 1930 have been the result, directly or indirectly, of the Second World War or of technological progress.

Introducing Britain since 1930

Who lives in Britain since 1930?

Subject facts

Since 1930 Britain has become more diverse in its make-up than ever before. The Second World War truly marked the end of the Empire, and Britain soon rushed to rid itself of the burden of its overseas possessions in the 1950s and

1960s. By no means all of this transition was carried out smoothly or without pain – genocide on the Indian sub-continent is perhaps the best example of this. But Britain found itself impoverished by the War, and searching for an identity and place in the new order of things. It was confused about its role in Europe, and took a long time in deciding whether to join the Common Market. Emigration to Australia and Canada was one escape for Britons seeking a post-War fresh start, and at the same time immigrants from the Commonwealth began to change the ethnic mix in Britain irrevocably. Slowly, Britain regained its place as one of the world's leading economies, and also showed a talent for technological innovation.

Timeline

1933	*Peak year for registered unemployed – just under 3 000 000.*
	Hitler becomes German chancellor.
1934	*30mph (45km/h) speed limit introduced on all roads.*
1936	*BBC makes its first TV broadcast.*
	King Edward VIII abdicates.
1937	*Frank Whittle makes the first jet engine.*
	Nylon manufactured.
1939	*First automatic washing machine goes on sale.*
	Germany invades Poland: the Second World War begins.
1944	*Education Act.*
1945	*Atomic bombs dropped on Japan; end of the Second World War.*
1946	*National Health Service set up.*
	New Towns Act.
	Bread rationing, not used during the War, introduced for the first time by a new Labour government.
1948	*Bread rationing ends.*
	The Empire Windrush lands the first coloured immigrants in Britain.
1950	*Sainsbury's first self-service store opens in Croydon.*
1951	*The Festival of Britain opens.*
1953	*The coronation of Elizabeth II in Westminster Abbey, June 2nd.*
	Hillary and Tensing the first to climb Mount Everest.
	First connections made between smoking and lung cancer.
1955	*ITV makes its first broadcast.*
1957	*The Treaty of Rome establishes the Common Market.*
1959	*First section of the M1 motorway opened.*
1960	*17 African colonies become independent in one year.*
1961	*Yuri Gagarin is the first man in space.*
1967	*First heart transplant performed by Barnard.*

Why do we need to know about Britain since 1930?
This period has a critical and immediate impact upon the lives of children in school, especially those who trace their roots to outside Britain. To understand the modern world, you have to study it.

How do we know about Britain since 1930?
This is the only topic studied at Key Stage 2 for which oral and eyewitness evidence exists. The period is within living memory, but it is also within the period of rapid advances in storage and retrieval of information, and this has added to the amount of evidence available. It is worth noting that, in spite of this wealth of evidence – artefacts, documents and the rest – and of people who can say 'I know because I was there', historians still argue over both the facts and their interpretation.

Vocabulary

The Blitz – a shortened version of the German *Blitzkrieg*, meaning 'lightning war'. Used to describe the intense bombing of British cities by the German airforce.
Doodlebug – the slang name for the powered V1 bomb invented by the Germans. A terror weapon used with little accuracy against cities. Also called the buzz-bomb.
GIs – General Infantryman or General Issue (slang) – term for an American serviceman.
Luftwaffe – the German airforce.
Prefab – temporary housing, post-1944, to meet the need caused by bomb damage. Factory pre-constructed and erected on site, 125 000 had been made by 1948.
Smog – intense mixture of smoke and fog that choked Britain's industrial cities, especially London, killing many. Led to the Clean Air Act of 1956.
Blackout – a law was passed during the War insisting that all outside lighting was switched off at night, and interior lighting had to be screened from the outside to deny navigational clues to enemy aircraft.
Barrage balloons – large balloons operated by winches and cables that were used to deter low-flying aircraft, particularly dive-bombers, from attacking particular targets such as factories and ports. They were often operated by women.
Adolf Hitler – was the leader (Fuhrer) of Germany during the War, and committed suicide when Berlin was captured.
Mussolini – was the wartime leader of Italy, and was called *Il Duce* ('the leader'). Shot by communist parties at the end of the War.

The Second World War

This National Curriculum topic is not intended to be a military study, but you do need to know the framework of military events on which the social history hangs.

Timeline

1939	*Britain declares war on Germany on September 3rd.* *Evacuation of children from the cities to country areas begins.*
1940	*Winston Churchill becomes Prime Minister.* *British and French troops (337 000) evacuated from Dunkirk after being defeated by the German army in Europe.* *RAF fights off the Luftwaffe in the Battle of Britain.* *The bombing of British cities begins (August) – the Blitz.*
1941	*Japanese make an unprovoked attack on the American fleet in Pearl Harbour.*
1942	*Turning point in the land war against Germany: British defeat the German army at El Alamein (North Africa).* *Russians defeat the Germans at the siege of Stalingrad.* *Greatest ever defeat of the British Army when Singapore surrenders to the Japanese.*
1944	*Allied armies land in Normandy (D-Day 6th June).*
1945	*VE Day (Victory in Europe – May).* *Atomic bombs dropped by the Americans on the Japanese cities of Hiroshima and Nagasaki.* *VJ Day (Victory against Japan – August).*

The Blitz

Although British servicemen fought in Europe, Africa, Asia and the seas across the globe, the biggest impact of the War on the majority of Britons was made by the German bombing raids upon Britain itself.

Failure to defeat the RAF in the Battle of Britain in 1940 led the Luftwaffe to turn its attention to civilian targets. This was partly to disrupt the industrial infrastructure of the nation, and partly to terrorize the population into submission. The bombing, most of which took place at night, was deadly and horrific, and caused some 60 284 civilian casualties. Of the 45 000 killed, nearly half lived in London, which took the brunt of these attacks. The peak year for casualties was 1940.

The population took shelter where it could find it. Public shelters were built, individuals constructed their own 'Anderson' shelters at home, and thousands of Londoners sought safety in the deep tunnels of the Underground railway system. In spite of its horrific nature, the bombing of civilians during the War has been shown to be largely ineffective. But the Luftwaffe's switch to civilian targets allowed the decimated RAF to recover from the Battle of Britain, and thus the threat of a German invasion was removed.

Evacuation

The evacuation of children to the comparative safety of the countryside proved to be a very significant social event. The intention was to save young lives and to boost the morale of the fighting men by reassuring them that their offspring were safe at home. Some children were sent by ship to Canada, but for the majority it was a case of internal exile. In the event there were significant unforeseen social effects as a result of thrusting many poor urban children on the rural population. The social classes mixed as never before.

When the German advance into Poland began, the arrangements were made to persuade parents living in the cities to allow their children (most were between the ages of 5 and 14) to make the journey away from the cities and into the countryside. The first wave of evacuation was a little premature, because nothing much by way of military incident happened at the beginning of the war. Consequently, many civilians miscalculated the extent of the dangers that bombing might bring. Many evacuees returned, and parents were very reluctant to be separated from their children again. This all changed when the Blitz began but by then, because large numbers of children had started to drift back to the cities, a second wave of evacuation had to begin.

In London, use was made of the Underground network to keep the assembling children away from the mainline stations, and they were taken to suburban stations to board trains to the more remote areas.

The logistical implications were enormous. Posters were displayed making people aware of the disruption to railway services that the evacuation would cause. Teachers, policemen, volunteers from the WRVS, and members of the WI were involved in escorting, feeding and caring for the travelling children.

What was not expected was the shock that would ensue when city children met country people. On a personal level, the experiences of the evacuees deposited on rural families ranged from loving and caring to the downright cruel but, as a nation, the experience was one that left a lasting impression. Malnourished, ill-clothed youngsters stirred the consciences of the well-to-do and country people in general, and this led to the support, from all classes, given to the social and welfare changes that were introduced after the War. Not all the evacuees returned home; this also injected new blood into rural communities and was another impetus to change.

In their own words

> *Please help me, I can still feel the quick beating of the children's hearts from the bombs dropping under half a mile from the house last Tuesday.*
> Father's letter pleading for a place in the
> country for his children. Wiltshire Record Office

Rationing

Sharing out essential food and other materials was shown to be a necessity in the First World War so the government was quick to introduce it in the Second. German submarine attacks upon merchant shipping threatened to starve the nation into submission because it was much more dependent upon overseas supplies for its basic needs then than it is now, when farming is so much more intense and productive. The U-boat attacks nearly succeeded and Britain's survival was threatened, but the government stuck to its policy. The diet of children and babies was controlled in a way that it had never been (or has been since) and was healthy and balanced. No one starved but there were shortages, and a black market in hard-to-obtain goods materialized.

Rationing was administered by the distribution of coupons, and the allowances were varied at different times during the War. The allowance for private fuel was withdrawn completely in 1942. Clothing was rationed (except hats and shoelaces) and this rationing, together with that of various foodstuffs and other domestic commodities, continued until 1954 – nine years after the war had finished.

The role of women and the Land Army

One of the most significant developments brought about by the War was the change in the role and status of women. Women were deeply involved in doing 'male' jobs in the First World War while the men were fighting, but when the war ended so did most of the jobs. Not so this time round: the change in how the role of women was perceived proved to be irrevocable.

Women were essential to the war effort; mainly it was a question of using women to do work at home so that men could be released to do the actual fighting. The range of work undertaken was much greater than in the First World War and there was no resistance to the involvement of women. There was a spirit of 'we are all in this together' that prevailed. Women even flew combat aircraft to and from the factories; they were crucial in the secret code-breaking work at Bletchey; they acted as spies; indeed, there was little that they did not do short of actually bearing arms and fighting.

Millions of women entered industry to replace men away at the front and to work on farms – the 'Land Army' was one of the most important roles undertaken. Women effectively took over agricultural production from men. The Women's Land Army was the only civilian service under direct government control, and 30 000 women volunteered for it at the start of the War.

The Home Guard

In the early summer of 1940, when fear of a German invasion had begun to grow, an appeal was issued by Sir Anthony Eden, the Secretary of State for War. Men between the ages of 17 and 65 who had not been conscripted were wanted to form a part-time military force that would take over the role of guarding key installations (such as railways and factories) from the regular army. They would also form an immediate-reaction delaying force should an invasion take place. The force was called the Local Defence Volunteers (LDV), or 'Look, Duck and Vanish' as their detractors said. After two months they were renamed the Home Guard and issued with boots.

They were easy to ridicule, especially in their infancy, as they were practically weaponless (broom handles and clubs were part of their 'armoury'), almost totally untrained, and rarely fit for military service. But this gradually changed: initially they were armed with second-rate weapons but later became properly equipped. They manned light anti-aircraft guns and searchlights and lost their 'useless' image. The Home Guard served until December 1944 when they were 'stood down'.

Although the Home Guard would never have been a serious opponent for the German Army it did, nevertheless, go on to play an important role at a time of extreme national danger. Its comic image has been perpetuated in the very successful television series *Dad's Army*.

Why you need to know these facts

The Second World War was the biggest war in history; its technological and social impact on Britain was enormous. It accelerated Britain's decline as a world power, vastly decreased the nation's wealth, totally undermined the Empire, and brought about irreversible social changes, particularly in relation to women in society. The role of the Commonwealth in the War underpinned the claim of immigrants who wished to live in Britain, and thus kick-started Britain's move towards a multi-ethnic society.

Amazing facts

● Britain was the only country in the War to conscript women, although most of them were not conscripted into the military. By 1943, all women from the age of 18 to 45 were conscripted to War work unless they had children under 14. War work could be in the forces (operating barrage balloons for example), the Land Army, or other War-related industry.

● During the Blitz road accidents increased due to the imposition of a night-time 'blackout'. In 1941 there were 9444 deaths caused by traffic accidents. The annual figure today, with greatly increased levels of traffic, is below 5000.

● Around three million children were evacuated from British cities.

● The blue paper bag used to hold the sugar ration led to that type of paper being called 'sugar paper' – the name commonly used for display and art paper in primary schools today.

Common misconceptions

All food was rationed.
It wasn't. Bread, flour, vegetables, fish, cheese, milk and coffee were never rationed during the War.

Teaching ideas

● Design a poster to encourage parents to evacuate their children to the country.

● After studying evacuees (perhaps read *Carrie's War* by Nina Bawden), pretend to be one and write a letter home to mum describing how you feel. Divide the class into groups and ask them to think about good experiences and bad.

● Compile a picture guide for RAF pilots to help them identify German aircraft (a small group activity).

● Using black paper (for silhouettes), and cotton wool (for

smoke and fire), make a large frieze showing the
devastation of the Blitz in London. Use St Paul's as a
landmark. You could add explanatory fact boxes to give
information on raids, casualty figures, dates and so on.

● Build model Anderson shelters using cardboard. Test
corrugated and un-corrugated versions for strength. Write
up your results for D&T.

● Undertake a class project to answer the question 'What
did women do in the War?' You could present the answers
as a radio programme, an assembly, a visual display or as a
computer presentation (using *PowerPoint* if you have it).

● Learn and perform some wartime songs. Why are so
many of them so weepy?

● Compare the biographies of wartime leaders given in
different sources. Compile brief biographies of your own.
(See Literacy Hour requirements for Year 6.)

The impact of social and technological changes

The Depression

Subject facts

A proportion of the population suffered considerable
hardship during the Depression of the early 1930s. This was
because the social and economic conditions were such that
the people most hit by industrial decline and the
concomitant unemployment were not financially supported
by the state to the extent that they would be today.

The trigger for the Depression was the crash of the
American stock market in 1929, the Wall Street Crash. The
reasons for this crash were complex and not fully
understood, but American consumers reacted by tightening
their belts so America's requirement for imported goods
rapidly decreased. Manufacturing nations, like Britain, soon
felt the impact of this drop in demand. Belt-tightening
became the order of the day and the British government cut
spending on just about everything in order to balance the
budget, causing suffering, particularly amongst the
unemployed. But because the prices of raw materials
dropped along with other prices, the standard of living of
those people actually in work rose. There was a boom in
housebuilding in some areas and the rate of public building
rose to 350 000 a year. This meant that the impact of the
Depression was not equally distributed across the country.

Steel, coal, and shipbuilding – all the old heavy industries
– were particularly badly hit. They had already been in a

state of decline due to the introduction of alternative power supplies (oil) and a lack of mechanization and investment that rendered these industries less competitive against the thrusting new economies of the Far East, Japan and India. Demand for British cotton decreased considerably; the coal industry lagged well behind its European competitors in introducing mechanization. Even by 1939 there were still 70 000 pit ponies down the mines in Britain and the proportion of mechanically extracted coal had only reached 60 per cent as against 97 per cent in Germany. A great deal of coal was still painfully hewn by hand.

The Depression brought down the second Labour government, and a National Government – a coalition with a Conservative majority but led by the Labour leader Ramsay MacDonald – took over. Teachers and other government employees had their pay cut, the dole was cut and began to be means-tested, and there was genuine poverty as a result. Photographs of the Jarrow marchers lend credence to the view that workers in the north suffered particularly, as the strain of hardship is visible on the faces of the marchers. Official figures show a peak in unemployment of just below 3 million in 1933, but the figure may have touched 3.75 million in 1932.

In the end, Britain spent its way out of Depression, largely because investment was needed to build up Britain's armed forces for anticipated conflict.

Post-War rebuilding: the start of the National Health Service

Although British war aims were simple and clear – victory against fascism – as the battles progressed and victory became a matter of time, so the feeling grew that we must be fighting for something more than mere victory; social change had to take place. The new post-War Britain had to be better than the Britain of before the War with its unequal distribution of wealth, dole queues, poverty, and under-educated and less than healthy masses. The state of many of the evacuees brought this to the front of the national consciousness – more than any other single event – although the deplorable fitness of many of the recruits into the forces also came as a shock. Pressure for change grew within the serving forces, where educational and political seminars were popular, but it ranged across the social spectrum. Even while the War was being persecuted the government set up working parties and committees to look into how to improve the nation's education system and its health service.

William Beveridge, previously the successful director of the London School of Economics, chaired a government committee of enquiry into the state of provision in the area of social welfare and health. This committee carried out a widespread investigation and looked at provision from company-run health services to the funding of GPs. In 1942 it issued a report on *Social Insurance and Allied Services* (The Beveridge Report), which in spite of sounding technical and tedious was nevertheless a seminal document. It turned out to be the catalyst for subsequent legislation that established the Welfare State.

Beveridge recommended a comprehensive scheme of social insurance to pay for a national scheme for health and welfare. In the first general election after the War, a Labour government was elected by a landslide with the expectation and desire for change. It planned for the National Health Service (NHS) to start in 1948, but its birth was subject to considerable pre-natal pain. Doctors had to be bribed to take part, mainly by allowing them to retain some private practice outside the NHS. Every service was intended to be free but the initial rush of overprescription and overuse quickly eroded the free service, although it still remains free in its essential services; a tribute to its creators. The NHS had to deal with a backlog of treatment that had built up over the years because people could not afford proper healthcare before its introduction. Nevertheless, it gradually contributed to improvements in the nation's health which, coupled with growing affluence, led to improvements in living standards and life expectancy during the 1950s and 1960s. The service consequently became a victim of its own success, with more and more demands being placed upon it – a problem that exists to this day.

The Festival of Britain and the coronation

Two memorable events of the post-War years, which perhaps seemed more significant at the time than they seem to be in retrospect, were the Festival of Britain and the coronation.

The Festival (opened in May 1951, the same month as the first *Goon Show*) was conceived as an event that would raise the nation's spirits and bring colour to the years made drab by war and rationing constraints. It was a national letting-down of the hair and was intended to contain echoes of the Great Exhibition of 1851 where there was a celebration of industrial and technological skill and a peep into the future. Festival of Britain stamps were issued, but the focal event was the South Bank Exhibition, with its

Dome of Discovery, Shot Tower, Skylon and Royal Festival Hall. The Millennium Dome and the millennium celebrations are the nearest modern equivalent events. Like these, the Festival had its opponents (most centred on the cost – £11 million) and its problems but it was, by and large, a success.

Thousands flocked to the South Bank. Parties of schoolchildren came from all over the country, many camping on the outskirts of London in places such as Slough. They were bussed in daily to the Festival to admire the modern machines, cars and other exhibits. Gremlin Grange was a higgledy-piggledy house that poked fun at what was considered to be bad architecture; there was a small zoo, and a Festival train (the Far Tottering and Oyster Creek Railway). Down the river the Battersea Funfair was one of the Festival's big successes, although the only lasting aspect of the Festival was the Royal Festival Hall which remains one of London's premier concert venues.

The coronation of Queen Elizabeth II was a true historical watershed. At the time it was seen as heralding a new 'Elizabethan Age' and there was expectation of a new era of greatness for Britain. In practice, the new age it heralded was the television age. Televisions were bought in their thousands specifically for the purpose of seeing the royal celebrations. The coronation acted as a trigger that set off the nation's love affair with 'the box'. Many people had their first experience of the flickering screen gathered in a neighbour's living room, watching the black and white images of the procession through the streets of London moving on what was, by modern standards, a tiny screen.

The Queen was crowned on June 2nd 1953 before a congregation of 8000 in Westminster Abbey. Three quarters of a million people, many from distant parts of the Commonwealth, lined the streets on what turned out to be a wet June day. Souvenirs abounded and schoolchildren were presented with coronation mugs by many local authorities. The Queen was transported in a gilded coach built in 1761, but newly renovated: as a concession to comfort, it was given rubber tyres.

New towns

The urge to rebuild a new and modern Britain to replace the bombed and depressed wastelands created by the ravages of war and the economic depression of the 1930s manifested itself in the concern with planning. The excesses of ribbon development were to be curbed, slums would be cleared and brave new worlds would rise in their place. The New Towns Act (1946) created new town development corporations that would extend existing villages and, with their extensive powers, build entirely new communities specially designed to cope with the so-called 'overspill' from the big cities, particularly London.

Within the London commuting area were built Basildon, Crawley, Stevenage and, latterly (1967), the largest: Milton Keynes. Other key new towns were Peterlee, Washington, Newton Aycliffe, Cwmbran, Cumbernauld, Corby, Telford and Skelmersdale. These developments ate up the countryside, and the opposition of the small communities that they destroyed, no matter how vigorously they campaigned, was simply swept aside. To many inhabitants, coming from decaying property in inner cities, the new homes were paradise. Even so, the new towns suffered from considerable crime and social problems stemming from the turbulence caused by the break-up of established urban communities; many new town dwellers missed their old tight-knit neighbourhoods.

Immigration and emigration

Although there is a sense in which Britain has always been a multi-ethnic nation, with a mix of Celts, Irish, Normans, Scandinavians, Huguenots and so on, until the 1950s, Britain was essentially a white European country. In 1948 the first Jamaican immigrants arrived on the ship *The Empire Windrush* (492 passengers and 18 stowaways), and this event marked the beginning of Britain becoming a multi-ethnic country.

Most immigrants claimed right of entry because they were Commonwealth citizens and many of the first contingents were mainly ex-servicemen who had fought in the Second World War. For political as well as practical reasons, Britain found it hard to refuse entry to those seeking to live here, although there was some opposition from the start. However, their arrival was not considered to be a major issue. (One civil servant is credited with having commented that after one British winter they would all go home.) But chance and need concentrated the immigrants into the poorer and often decaying working-class areas of the inner cities. The accompanying disruption and social strain triggered a debate about immigration controls. Opinion polls taken in 1961 showed that 90 per cent of the public were in favour of them, so in 1962 an Immigration Act introduced a quota system. Alongside this Act were Acts against racial discrimination. The Institute of Race Relations was set up in 1958.

In the years following the initial period of immigration, successive British governments have emphasized its positive side. The events of the 1950s initiated the biggest social and cultural change for many centuries and Britain's population now contains several million black Britons. This has enriched the culture and changed Britain's perspective on the world. Britain has also been forced to face up to the moral and religious issues that arise when cultural differences have to be faced. It has also had to struggle with the issue of identity. The British are still divided, for example, on the issue of Europe, and are not always clear which cricket team they should support! (A recent best-selling book by Jeremy Paxman focused entirely on what it is to be 'English' – not a question that would have been thought difficult to answer in 1939.)

Post-War Britain was also a time of accelerated emigration. There was a great deal of going (and coming back in many instances) to places such as Canada and Australia. There were many incentives to go, not only the desire to make a fresh start in a new world, but also there were assisted passage schemes to get the emigrants off to a good start.

Technology and social change

Television was the big innovation of the 1950s, but one must not forget that throughout the 1930s and the War years, people all over the country were avid listeners to the wireless. *ITMA (It's That Man Again)* was as keenly listened to as *EastEnders* is watched today. The world's first regular television service, the BBC, began broadcasting from Alexandra Palace in London in November 1936, but it was not until after the coronation coverage that television programmes really started to develop. In 1958 television licences (8 million) exceeded radio-only licences (6.5 million) for the first time. Radio programmes such as *Children's Hour* continued to attract children to the stories of *Toytown* and *Larry the Lamb,* and the mellifluous tones of David Davis enthralled children with the weekly serial, the *Tales of Narnia* or *The Eagle of the Ninth.* Their parents were equally hooked on *Take it From Here, The Billy Cotton Band Show, The Archers* and *The Goon Show. The Third Programme* (now Radio Three) was started in 1946 to accompany *The Home Service* (which was renamed Radio Four in 1967).

Television's first stars were the newsreaders, people like MacDonald Hobley and Sylvia Peters, and the puppet Muffin the Mule. Television programmes such as *Newsreel* and

Saturday Night at the London Palladium were watched by millions, as was *The Interlude*, a strange endlessly looping film clip of activities such as throwing a pot, inserted when things went wrong with the live broadcasts – which they often did.

Cinema and records
Cinema-going was at its peak in the 1930s and 1940s, and remained popular through the beginnings of television. Saturday morning pictures were attended by millions of children and could be a fairly riotous occasion. Films such as *High Noon*, *The Guns of Navarone* and *Fantasia* were big hits in the 1950s. Changes in the production of records (not discs) and record players saw the end of the wind-up players and 78rpm records, and the introduction of 45s and radiograms in the 1950s.

The refrigerator and supermarkets
One of the most influential post-War technological changes was the introduction of the refrigerator to most homes. The technology was not new, but growing affluence and the development of the old war industries to satisfy home domestic consumption generated a need which industry was able to meet. Patterns of shopping therefore began to change. The daily walk to the shops to fetch fresh food was made unnecessary by the 'fridge' and the growing number of car owners meant that more shopping could be carried in one trip than previously. Small local shops began to close and bigger ones took their place.

The first supermarket opened by Sainsburys was in Croydon in 1950. It was the beginning of a revolution.

The motor car and travel
In 1939 Britain possessed more tarmac road for its area than any other country in the world, over 270 000km (180 000 miles) of road. Its railway network was also extensive – around 30 000km (20 000 miles) of track and 20 000 locomotives – and was reasonably efficient. During the War there was a shift towards rail for the transportation of goods that resulted in a 77 per cent increase in rail traffic and brought the railways to breaking point by 1945. As part of the Labour government's initiatives when elected in 1945, the railways were nationalized (1948), and road haulage and the inland waterways were brought under the control of the British Transport Commission in an attempt to create an integrated transport policy.

But as car ownership increased an axe was taken to the

railway network, which seemed absolutely necessary at the time, although it has been questioned since. Under the 'Beeching Cuts' in 1963, 2000 rural stations were closed. Steam had already had its day and the last steam train was built in 1967.

In 1950 there were 2 307 000 car owners; by 1960 this had risen to 5 650 000. This was the beginning of a trend that still continues. Traffic congestion is not new, for in the 1930s places like Oxford Street virtually ground to a halt even though there were far fewer vehicles in those days. Accidents were at a level far higher than today and resulted in a number of traffic controls. The first driving tests were introduced in 1934 and traffic lights, first seen in 1925, became more widespread.

Travelling began to be a pastime that was no longer the preserve of the rich. In the 1930s it was by bike and foot that many explored the world (growth years for the Youth Hostel Association and the years of bitter conflict over access rights between ramblers and landowners). In the post-War years it was the train excursion initially, then the motor car, and the beginnings of foreign travel by air. Britain invented the world's first jet airliner in the 1950s – the De Havilland Comet. The arterial road and the bypass were the invention of the 1930s, and the motorway the child of the 1950s and 1960s.

Why you need to know these facts

Britain of the early 21st century – multi-ethnic, sans-Empire, affluent and hi-tech – has its origins in the last century. To understand today, particularly the multi-ethnic nature of Britain and the industrial changes that have taken place, you need to understand these origins.

Amazing facts

● Between 6 and 7 million British people became dependent upon the dole during the Depression.
● Wigs, false teeth, glasses and even prescriptions were entirely free when the NHS began.
● The Minister for Town and Country Planning, Lewis Silkin, had sand put in his petrol tank by opponents to the building of the new town of Stevenage when he visited the area. The station sign was changed to 'Silkingrad'.
● In one of the peak early years for immigration (1961), 113 000 people arrived in Britain from India, Pakistan and the West Indies.

The Festival of Britain took place in London.
In fact, it was a nationwide event with processions, fetes and street concerts, entertainments and parties locally initiated all over the country.

● Compile a class dictionary (illustrated) of key words associated with social change in this period: The Festival of Britain, smog, new towns, the Jarrow March and the Beeching Axe among others.
● Make large cardboard cut-outs of identifiable groups from the period. Research carefully groups such as spivs, teddy boys, mods, rockers, mini-skirted swingers from the 1960s. Write descriptions saying who, when and even why.
● On an outline map of the world, show the flow of post-War immigration and emigration.
● Who were the pop stars grandma and grandad enjoyed? Make a presentation based on interviews and recordings.
● Have a debate about the advantages and disadvantages of reopening old railway lines. Alternatively, do a similar exercise on the value (or not) of the building of motorways.
● If you had a Festival of Britain today, what would you have in it? Devise a programme for the event.
● Watch a film made in the period. Divide the children into groups to note particular social differences from today. Look at dress, transport, hairstyles, shops, interior decoration and design and so on.
● Invite outside speakers to tell the children how they enjoyed themselves 'in those days' – when they were 11 years old. You could choose someone in their early twenties and someone over sixty, for example.
● Make a technology timeline showing the main innovations since 1930.

Resources

The sheer quantity of material can make it difficult to cope with this topic, but on the other hand you have plenty to chose from. Don't miss what is readily to hand: people, for example the school caretaker who was an evacuee, great grandad who fought with the army and so on. There will be local evidence to hand as well: a War memorial in the park, a local museum, an air-raid shelter preserved as a museum, homes and buildings, or a loft full of 1950s toys and redundant domestic equipment. Ask the children to do their own search for evidence.

Children's books

The events of the mid-century have produced a rich harvest of children's historical fiction and the list continues to grow. Do check that you are comfortable with the text before reading to your children, or you may have parental complaints to deal with (Robert Westall's books often contain swearing). A few to consider are:

Carrie's War by N Bawden (Penguin) – a classic about evacuees. A BBC video is available.

Goodnight Mr Tom by Michelle Magorian (Puffin) – a well-loved weepy about the evacuation of a deprived child to the country. Also a TV drama.

When the siren wailed by N Streatfeild (Armada).

The Machine Gunners by R Westall (Macmillan) – watch out for the language.

The Silver Sword by I Serraillier (Penguin) – another classic, multi-layered and not to be missed.

Rose Blanche by C Gallaz (J Cape) – a powerful picture book with a difference; it deals with concentration camps.

Multimedia

Documentary and visual evidence is vast. There are a number of CD-ROMs available that contain excellent material (the best strategy is to consult a reliable catalogue) and some wonderful collections of photographs, documents and newspaper extracts. Don't forget music – not only collections of popular songs but music inspired by the period. It is also worth checking with your local newspaper to see what they have in their archives. Here are a few examples to explore:

Children of the Blitz by Robert Westall (Macmillan) – memories of the wartime experiences of children – superbly quotable to recapture the feeling of the time.

A Child's War by M Brown (Sutton publishing) – full of information and evidence of growing up on the Home Front.

Union Jack: A Scrapbook of British Forces Newspapers 1939–45 (HMSO).

London at War The Hulton-Deutsch Collection (Quoin Publishing) – wonderful collection of photographs.

I'll Be Seeing You (EMI) – a collection of World War II songs.

Wartime Women by D Sheridan (Mandarin) – mass observation anthology – quotable extracts.

Countrywomen on the Land by G Nelson – rural life in the 1930s – more useable extracts.
Ready Steady Go! by Chris Tarrant (Hamlyn) – a wonderful anthology of quotations and photographs, excellent for history and the Literacy Hour.

1950s and 1960s

Ration Book Recipes: Some Food Facts 1939–1954 by G Corbishley (English Heritage).
The day they took the children by B Wicks (Bloomsbury) – personal memories of evacuees.
The Home Front: Documents relating to life in Britain, 1939–1945 (Imperial War Museum).
Britain Since 1930: resource pack (Collins) – a collection of pictures and photocopiables for use in the classroom.
The Best of Times by Alison Pressley (Michael O'Mara Books) – plenty of oral evidence and pictures of the fifties.
Children's reference books on the period are also plentiful but the list does change as titles go out of print, so check with your local library service or publisher's catalogues.

Background reading for teachers is again plentiful. You might start with the very readable *British Society Since 1945* A Marwick (Penguin), which is a scholarly social history; and *The Ordeal of Total War* G Wright (Harper Row), which goes beyond battles to examine what mass war means in the industrial age. The highly acclaimed *Never Again* Peter Hennessy (Vintage) is a very detailed account of the immediate post-War years.

Chapter 12

Local history study

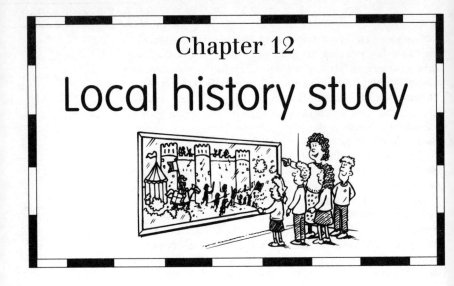

Teaching a local history topic can be both the most daunting and the most exciting and rewarding of topics. It is daunting because, depending on the choice of subjects, it can require a substantial amount of effort and knowledge to make the topic come alive. But this need not be the case. What you choose to study is the most important decision you have to make. Given a good subject, the topic can come alive like no other because it is local, easy to link to the children's experience, and can lead to real, and sometimes even original, historical enquiry.

Why you need to know these facts

For obvious reasons there is not one single body of historical knowledge that the children must learn, although they will acquire *a* body of knowledge during this topic. Any historical knowledge from any period of British history might, of course, be applicable to your local study, which is why we cannot give you lists of facts here.

First you need to know where to start. The choice of topics is wide and you have been given the opportunity to put back in to the curriculum favourite topics that the National Curriculum has bypassed or ones for which you are particularly well-resourced. Consider studying early history if you live near an interesting site (such as Avebury or Maiden Castle); or the English Civil War (especially if you have a particularly appropriate location like Newbury or Newark nearby); or the Georgians (Bath or Buxton); the Great Plague (London or Eyam); or Isambard Kingdom Brunel (Bristol, or anywhere on the Great Western line). There are many exciting possibilities. Investigate your area, talk to local people, visit the reference library, or simply look around you.

The parameters that define your topic choice are:
● It must have a local dimension – local can be interpreted fairly broadly (not necessarily a precise place or within a set number of yards), so it could range from the choice of a wide geographical area to that of a particular building or person in an area;
● It could fit into a single period of British history (from within or outside National Curriculum topics) or range over several periods.

You must study:
● Change over a long period of time (an aspect of the locality);
● A significant national or local event or development that affected the locality;
● A significant individual who affected the locality.

Shops and shopping

Teaching ideas

Look at what has happened in the local High Street over a set period of time. Compare grandma's day with today. Look for the legacy of previous shopping practices – ethnic foods, restaurants and so on.

Hospitals and doctors
Start with a 'sick care' map of the area showing hospitals, doctors, ambulance stations and clinics. Trace the history of medical provision.

Place names and street names
Walk the streets. Study maps. Who or what are the streets named after? (There is usually logic behind the street names of even a modern estate. Can you tease out the logic behind the choices?) Tell the story of the events that gave names to the streets or places (look, for example, at The Crimean War or industrial sites – 'Brick Kiln Lane').

Football or other sporting clubs
Plot the history in the town.

Monuments and statues

These can provide excellent starting points. Famous local or national heroes open the door to the study of major historical events. Plaques on the sides of buildings can start the children on a trail of exploration. Check to see if the school has one, just in case.

A historic building

Is the school worthy of study? Perhaps there is a stately home nearby? What about the market or Town Hall?

A local newspaper

Some local newspapers have quite a long history themselves. Through them you can retell the story of the town over a period of time.

A market history

There are many markets around Britain and many old market towns. Some markets no longer actually exist or have merged into a local fair. Check for possibilities.

Transport and travel

Coaching inns, canals, railway lines, stations, airfields, old trackways, turnpikes, toll gates and so on can all be wonderful starting points.

Hedges and parish boundaries

Specialist knowledge may be needed but the project would involve active research, the use of old maps and plenty of fieldwork. You could carry out a hedge dating exercise.

Bridges, castles and churches

Other major constructions may be equally useful doorways to the past in your locality. If you have an ancient crossing point, a castle or medieval church, then you are fortunate.

A new estate

It may seem a barren land historically but ask the question – What was it like before? Until very recently estate roads usually followed old field boundaries (use maps) because land was sold in field 'parcels'. Check old photographs, the local press and museum.

A local traditional event

This could be anything, like the annual handing out of 'buns' at the almshouses in Bedworth, Warwickshire or the Guy Fawkes celebrations at Lewes in Sussex.

Perhaps more than any other unit in the curriculum at Key Stage 2, this one demands adequate resources. This does not necessarily mean that you need piles of specialist material or knowledge, but you do need *appropriate* resources. So if you don't have the material, choose a different topic. There is nothing to be gained (except pain) from studying a topic that is inadequately resourced.

One excellent resource is the experience of others. Check what other teachers in your school have done before you. Watch the educational press for case studies that you might emulate. The magazine of English Heritage, *Heritage Learning,* often has good ideas or illustrated case studies. The magazines of the Historical Association, *Teaching History* and *Primary History,* are worth looking at. Scholastic also publishes a range of magazines that often contain useful material. *National Trust Education News* and the magazines of the *TES* are other possible sources.

Books

For books and materials on specific periods you should consult the usual sources – starting with the school library. The following publications offer helpful advice and ideas that may be relevant to the topic of your choice:

History in the School Grounds by Jaqui Dean (Southgate).

Street Furniture by Henry Aaron (Shire Publications) – there are over 100 titles in this series and the list will repay examination.

A Sense of History, Local History Teacher's Guide, by Sallie Purkis (Longman) – although a little dated in National Curriculum terms, it is a useful and encouraging book.

A Teacher's Guide to Using Listed Buildings by Crispin Keith (English Heritage).

A Teacher's Guide to Using School Buildings by Sallie Purkis (English Heritage).

Using Documents by Ian Davies and Chris Webb (English Heritage) – there are also other useful titles in this series.

Using the Historic Environment, Practical Ideas and Activities for Teachers (English Heritage).

The Ordnance Survey Complete Guide to the Battlefields of Britain by David Smurthwaite (HMSO) – concise and well-illustrated, see what applies to your area.

Local history study is a widespread hobby and there will almost certainly be a local history society near you that can provide you with expertise or advice. Because the study of local history is so popular, there are a fair number of reference books on the subject.

Local History in England by W G Hoskins (Longman, 3rd edition) – although a little dated, still a masterly, enthusiastic and readable introduction to the topic.

The Concise Oxford Dictionary of English Placenames by E Ekwall (Oxford University Press) – a standard reference book.

Suburban Style, The British Home, 1840–1960 by Helena Barrett and John Phillips (Macdonald Orbis) – an indispensible reference book if your study includes domestic architecture, or a difficult study of a housing estate, well-illustrated.

History
INDEX